GULLAH GEECHEE HERITAGE
in the
GOLDEN ISLES

GULLAH GEECHEE HERITAGE
in the
GOLDEN ISLES

AMY LOTSON ROBERTS & PATRICK J. HOLLADAY, PhD

Foreword by Dr. Melanie R. Pavich and Professor Tyler E. Bagwell

THE
History
PRESS

Published by The History Press
Charleston, SC
www.historypress.com

First published 2019

Manufactured in the United States

ISBN 9781467141185

Library of Congress Control Number: 2019939731

Notice: The information in this book is true and complete to the best of our knowledge. It is offered without guarantee on the part of the authors or The History Press. The authors and The History Press disclaim all liability in connection with the use of this book.

*This book is respectfully dedicated to all the elders
and Gullah Geechee people in Glynn County.*

Contents

CONTENTS

FOREWORD

Gullah Geechee Heritage in the Golden Isles is a book every resident and vacationer needs in their personal library. A book like *Gullah Geechee Heritage in the Golden Isles* is long overdue and a welcome addition to a fuller and richer understanding of this special place. The Golden Isles have been home to many over the centuries—many whose lives and contributions remain hidden in the shadows. Yet they are vital to the rich fabric of history and culture that continues to draw us to this beautiful and mysterious coastal region. It is far too easy to live, work and play on the Georgia coast and ignore its roots in the institution of slavery and the essential contributions of the enslaved and their descendants to its development and its riches, both economically and culturally. The stories and the voices in this volume help us to know and to remember.

Two preeminent scholars of the region, St. Simons Island native and historian Amy Roberts and researcher and academic Patrick Holladay, skillfully guide the reader around the islands and mainland using untold stories and rare photographs to surprise and captivate. The authors carefully detail the language, traditions and crafts of the Gullah Geechee and highlight important Gullah Geechee events and people of African descent who influenced the Golden Isles.

Through letters, diaries and other primary sources available to researchers, much can be learned of the lives of the rich and powerful. Yet how do we access the experiences of those who leave little such evidence of their lives? In part, it is through books like this one that we can learn of a vital culture built by the Gullah Geechee in coastal Georgia. It is a culture that valued and emphasized family life. When they could not hold their families together, they formed kinship networks and family units within the communities in which they lived. That sense of family and community has strong and powerful roots that live on today. They developed a deep culture in terms of work, language, foodways, religion, music, storytelling, arts and crafts that reaches back to their homelands in Africa and has been passed down and is generously shared through yearly events like the Georgia Sea Islands Festival. Even though they were forbidden basic literacy and numeracy when enslaved, the Gullah Geechee, like African Americans throughout the South, valued education and, as soon as they could, built schools like the Harrington School on St. Simons Island. All of this and more was the prelude for what came with and after emancipation even in a South determined to drastically limit their citizenship and freedom. African Americans' desire for education, citizenship in the fullest sense, land, professions, work, the power to determine the course of their lives and a chance for their children to have a better future grew out of and on the foundations that were built during slavery.

Learn about the tragic bravery that took place on St. Simons Island in 1803 at Ibo Landing when captured Africans drowned themselves in Dunbar Creek rather than be enslaved. Find out about the *Wanderer*, one of the last slave ships to come to America when it anchored off Jekyll Island in 1858. Today, descendants of *Wanderer* captives still live on St. Simons Island and other parts of the Golden Isles. Discover why the millionaire newspaper publisher Robert Abbott erected a monument near the ruins of Fort Frederica and uncover the stories behind Hazel's Café, Bessie Jones and the Sea Island Singers and NFL Hall of Famer and professional actor Jim Brown.

Jekyll Island history devotees will surely recognize many of the names in this book and will be enlightened by tales of the vibrant black community known as Red Row that once thrived during the Jekyll Island Club period. Earl Hill, golf caddy in the 1920s for the exclusive club, became a skilled golfer, and as an adult, he helped organize a professional golf event on Jekyll Island called the Southeastern Golf Tournament. Prize money for the first tournament came from an Otis Redding Jr. concert. In this book, stories about African American leaders are conveyed, and bibliophiles will learn about two early Jekyll Island State Park homeowners: Dr. J. Clinton Wilkes and Genoa Martin. Martin served as the director of the Selden Recreational Park and attracted entertainers like Duke Ellington,

Cab Calloway and James Brown to Brunswick for sold-out concert performances.

From the islands to the mainland, readers will be fascinated by the insights provided by Amy Roberts and Patrick Holladay in their book *Gullah Geechee Heritage in the Golden Isles*.

Discover the unique legacy African culture has bestowed on the area and plan your visit to the heritage locations vividly described within these pages, including the Historic Harrington School, the *Wanderer* Memory Trail and the endangered architecture of Needwood Church. I urge every Golden Isles sojourner, whether permanent or simply a traveler, to obtain their copy and delve into the exciting stories and places described within this seminal work. You are invited to enter into this history, these stories, this world in *Gullah Geechee Heritage in the Golden Isles*. While this history, these stories and this world are written on the land and water, and in the lives and hearts of its people, we might miss all of it; it might otherwise remain elusive, unknown. We would be much the poorer, for this is not merely the heritage of the people who inhabit this coast but *our* heritage. The Golden Isles are not peripheral to the larger story of the Americas but a rich and essential chapter that should remain in the shadows no more. We are grateful to Amy Roberts and Patrick Holladay for connecting us to this past, these people and a larger, more inclusive world—to a better understanding of who we are.

TYLER E. BAGWELL
Author of *The Jekyll Island Club* and
Producer of *The Wanderer* GPB television special

MELANIE R. PAVICH, PhD
Penfield College
Mercer University

PREFACE

The contents of this book focus on Gullah Geechee heritage assets of the Golden Isles of Georgia. The book is an imaginative guide and historical narrative alive with accounts that describe places of cultural and heritage importance. Many descriptions come directly from people who were directly involved with the sites and attractions (or have intimate knowledge of the oral histories) written about in this book.

Read about, and hopefully visit, Ibo (Ebo or Igbo) Landing, the site of a mass suicide in protest to slavery; the Abbott Memorial, erected by Robert Abbott (who was born on St. Simons and later rose to prominence as the owner of the *Chicago Defender* newspaper) for his family; the Historical Harrington School, the only surviving one-room school on St. Simons Island; First African Baptist Church of St. Simons, which was established in 1859; and the tabby slave cabins of Hamilton Plantation.

Of importance will be the people woven into the stories of the places— people like Deaconess Alexander, Hall of Fame NFL player Jim Brown, Neptune Small, Hazel Floyd, the Georgia Sea Island Singers and more. Also of interest are Risley High School, Selden Park and Normal School, the Historic Greenwood Cemetery, Needwood Baptist Church, the Wanderer Memory Trail and the Red Row (i.e., servants' quarters) of the Jekyll Island Club, among many others. Sit back and learn, visualize and take this journey into local history and culture.

ACKNOWLEDGEMENTS

We would like to thank everyone in the Gullah Geechee community, the St. Simons African American Heritage Coalition, the Friends of the Harrington School and all our friends and families who work with the Coalition and the preservation of the Historic Harrington School. Also, thank you to all the other local groups working on heritage preservation and cultural continuation. Thank you to everyone who provided stories and had a hand in helping shape this work. Finally, to our Lord and Savior Jesus Christ; through Him all things are possible.

PART I

An Introduction to the History of the Golden Isles

Gullah Geechee Heritage

The Gullah Geechee people live in what many around the country or the world consider the "Lowcountry" of the southern United States, which is the low-lying coastal areas and barrier islands of the region. As some from that community say, they came to the United States on an "unplanned trip," primarily from West Africa. Originally, the Gullah Geechee people were brought to the New World in the transatlantic slave trade of the eighteenth and nineteenth centuries. They were captured from West African countries such as modern-day Angola, Senegal, Gambia, Sierra Leone and Liberia, which was an area known as the Rice Coast or Windward Coast,[1] and down to the Gold Coast of Ghana.[2] There were a number of West African tribes that were targeted and enslaved, including the people of the Rice Coast such as the Baga (Guinea), Fula (Nigeria, Guinea, Senegal), Kissi (Guinea, Sierra Leone, Liberia), Kpelle (Liberia), Limba (Sierra Leone), Mandika (Mali), Mende (Sierra Leone), Susu (Guinea, Sierra Leone), Temne (Sierra Leone), Vai (Liberia, Sierra Leone) and Wolof (Senegal, Gambia).[3]

One major area for trade in enslaved West African people was a fortified building on Bunce Island at the end of the Sierra Leone River in Sierra Leone. While there were around forty or so of these slave castles along the coast of West Africa, Bunce Island was by far the busiest with thousands of men, women and children passing through it on their way to a life of slavery in America.[4] The Gullah Geechee people, as descendants of enslaved Africans, come from various ethnic groups of mainly West and some Central Africa, as were mentioned earlier. These West Africans were brought to the New World and forced to work on the plantations of coastal South Carolina, Georgia, North Carolina and Florida. Gullah Geechee people have retained many aspects of their African heritage due to the geographic barriers of the coastal landscape and the strong sense of place and family of Gullah Geechee community members.

Today, according to the Gullah Geechee Cultural Heritage Corridor (a U.S. National Heritage Area),[5] the language and culture of Gullah Geechee people encompasses coastal areas and barrier Sea Islands from Pender County, North Carolina, to St. Johns County, Florida. The Gullah Geechee Cultural Heritage Corridor traditions are explained by the National Park Service:

> *This heritage is reflected within their naming traditions, linguistic patterns/ African vocabulary, worldview, philosophy, African religious syncretism, ring-shouts, sweetgrass basket weaving, mortar & pestle use, diet/cooking methods, carving traditions, fishing methods (net making and casting), quilting patterns (African symbolism), rice cultivation, and storytelling traditions.*[6]

Gullah Geechee people are believed to be the only speakers of true African American Creole language in the continental United States. Food, music, storytelling, family, language, African heritage, crafts, fishing, agriculture (especially the growing of rice) and a celebration of culture and people are all part of the fabric of the Gullah Geechee culture. The Gullah Geechee people were also allowed to practice their own religion, and isolation created a deep sense of kinship among the members of the community. Gullah Geechee culture remained a pure culture because of this isolation. It was not until the early to mid-1900s that bridges to the mainland from the various Sea Islands were built. No Gullah Geechee traveled from his or her island without a boat, and visitation from the mainland was minimal. Enslaved West Africans working on rice plantations formed a unique identity and foodways, among many other indigenous characteristics. Gullah Geechee culture has held more Africanisms (or a cultural feature that is considered typically African) than other African American communities in the United States.

The Gullah Geechee are separated from other African Americans because of their language, customs, traditions, culture and heritage that are largely connected to West Africa and the diaspora (i.e., the scattering of people from their native homeland). While there is no overwhelming consensus of how the name "Gullah Geechee" came to be, it may be derived from geographic locations of West Africa. First, the term "Gullah" could be interpreted from Angola[7] in the Congo. Second, Gola is an ethnic group living on the border between Sierra Leone and Liberia in West Africa, and Gola could be reimagined as Gullah. The name "Geechee" may come from an African tribe living on the border between Guinea and Liberia who were known as Kissi, which is pronounced *Geezee*. Other linguists have suggested that the name Geechee comes from the Ogeechee River, which flows through the state of Georgia in what was once Creek Indian land. Another thought on the origin of Gullah is the Spanish word *Guale*, which was the Spanish term

Gullah Geechee family with a wagon. *"Negro slaves 1862 Edisto Island, S.C. (plantation of James Hopkinson)." Library of Congress.*

for the coastal Native Americans. While the two Native American derivations are interesting, it is more likely that the West Africans would have referred to themselves with terms from their homeland.

The Gullah Geechee culture arose from the numerous West African tribes that were brought together on the coastal and Sea Islands of the southeastern United States. There was a commonality among them that helped them bond and begin the roots of the Gullah Geechee culture.

These West Africans who worked on the coastal plantations of North Carolina, South Carolina, Georgia and Florida were targeted as slaves because of their rice heritage and intellectual knowledge of rice cultivation. The enslaved blacks had a deep and intricate knowledge of these systems from their own agricultural practices at home, so they were captured and brought to the United States in ever-increasing numbers.[8] This knowledge was a science that included engineering, agronomy and even astronomy because the people had to know the cycles of tides, which were instrumental in flooding the rice fields with water. By the 1700s, a system of reservoirs, impoundments and irrigation using ocean tides had been established along the South Carolina and Georgia coasts that made rice a prized commodity. Sea Island cotton (a longer, thinner type of cotton) and indigo (which was one of the biggest commodity crops in the coastal United States in the late 1700s)[9] were also grown to diversify the plantations.

Gullah Geechee people retained many aspects of their culture due to the geographic barriers that isolated these Sea Island communities. Isolation is an important point of emphasis to truly begin to understand how the Gullah Geechee culture formed and survived over such a long period of time. It was isolation that strengthened the individualistic nature of the culture. Due to the difficult climate, risk of disease and dangers of venomous snakes, alligators and other animals, the Gullah Geechee plantation slave owners often stayed off the islands for long periods of time. This allowed a more autonomous life than is generally thought about for slaves in historic southern plantations like the cotton plantations. Although Gullah Geechee people traveled between nearby islands and the mainland, few outsiders entered the Gullah Geechee communities, particularly after the Civil War.

The mention of the Civil War brings to mind the horrific conflict over slavery and all that enslavement of human beings entailed. One generally thinks of the plantation system of the Deep South and the grueling sunrise-to-sunset toil that enslaved people endured in fields of cotton. This type of plantation system was much different for the slaves who worked on the rice, cotton, indigo and cane plantations of the Sea Islands. These people (who

Gullah Geechee workers in the cotton field. *Library of Congress.*

were the Gullah Geechee) worked their days on something that was known as a task system, which was a set of duties to be completed in a certain amount of time.

Gullah Geechee people were given more autonomy than slaves in other regions of the Southeast because the schedule of tasks, when completed, allowed people to grow their own produce and livestock. They were free to spend time crafting products like sweetgrass baskets and cast nets, hunt, fish and even sell their goods to make money for themselves.[10] White slave owners did not venture to the islands often because of the harsh conditions, fear of disease and sickness, as well as the perceived variety of dangers from animals and insects.

Crafts and Traditions

Gullah Geechee craftsmanship was superb and included numerous types of handmade items. Many Gullah Geechee craft traditions were important for day-to-day life and include sweetgrass basket "sewing" (i.e., weaving of marsh grass), cast net making (generally a circular net that is thrown to catch fish), smoking mullet and other seafood, quilting (often to make use of many small pieces of fabric), blending herbal medicines and potash (ashes that come from burning wood and plants) and soap making. Gullah Geechee craftsmen were instrumental in jobs like barrel making, carpentry, boat building, blacksmithing, brick making/masonry and as kitchen cooks.

Above: Gullah Geechee ladies at market. *The Miriam and Ira D. Wallach Division of Art, Prints and Photographs. Photography Collection, the New York Public Library. "Oyster and fish women, Charleston, S.C." The New York Public Library Digital Collections, 1870.*

Opposite: Sweetgrass baskets on display at Geechee Kunda in Riceboro, Georgia. *Patrick Holladay.*

Perhaps the most iconic craft tradition of the Gullah Geechee people is the weaving (or what Gullah Geechees call *sewing*) of sweetgrass (or coiled) baskets. The baskets were originally used in West Africa for mainly utilitarian purposes like winnowing rice and other household chores. In today's world, these baskets have become an art form and a valuable commodity for sale (although even in the slavery era the baskets were sold to non–Gullah Geechee people).

Another important tradition was Watch Night. This was a practice of commemorating the night of the Emancipation Proclamation put forth by President Abraham Lincoln that gave freedom to all enslaved people.

Storytelling

Storytelling is a large part of Gullah Geechee culture. The most well known of these are the Uncle Remus tales, which often revolve around the character of Br'er Rabbit. In popular culture, these were made famous with the Disney movie *Song of the South*. In the Uncle Remus stories, the animals would use tricks and guiles to outwit the stronger or dominant characters in the story. These were metaphors for freedom and came from the cultures of enslaved West Africans. Storytelling is an important element in Gullah Geechee families for it was in sharing these stories through generations that they were able to keep their family histories alive.

Food

The Gullah Geechee people have particularly distinctive foods, dishes and foodways (where food and culture meet to create unique history, heritage and the experience of shared culinary traditions). There is a marked intersection and linkage between West African–based cuisine and that of Gullah Geechee people. The proximity to the coast and life on islands lends itself inextricably to fishing, crabbing and gathering seafood.[11]

Beans, peas, okra, yams, peppers, peanuts, benne (sesame seeds), seafood, smoked fish (mullet), shrimp, oysters, grits and others are all longtime staples in Gullah Geechee dishes. Pilau or perlow, Hoppin' John and red rice all are one-pot or one-dish meals that are familiar to anyone eating on the southern U.S. coast. Many Gullah Geechee dishes are one-pot meals and come from the practice of combining what was on hand, and also sharing among families, to stretch what was available to feed more people. To further stretch their food, the enslaved Africans' communal (one-pot) dishes used game and "cast-off" parts like pig feet, jowls, heads and chitlins or the intestine of the animal. Other foods that became part of the menu were corn grits, squash and tomatoes that were learned from Native Americans who lived in the region and shared their knowledge of foods.

It is sometimes said by locals of the Sea Islands from North Carolina to Florida that rice is included in every Gullah Geechee meal. Rice was introduced to America in the 1600s. Rice plantations in Georgia were very plentiful and big business. Somewhere in the neighborhood of twenty-five thousand acres of Georgia coast were once planted in rice. Growing rice was a thankless and back-breaking work that followed the seasons and year cycles of cultivation, levee construction, digging, sowing and harvesting with a sickle. To prepare the rice to be ready for eating, it was first laid out on the ground and beaten to break the rice from the stalk. During this task, the slaves sang the "Flail Song" in order to stir up the wind to help them. The lyrics sang out:

Gullah Geechee fishermen. *Gullah oysterman on Hilton Head Island, SC. in 1904. American Museum of Natural History, Digital Special Collection.*

Blow, Tony, blow; O blow, Tony; blow, Tony; blow, Tony, blow!
I whip dis' rice an' I whip 'em so; blow, Tony, blow!
I whip dis' rice an' I whip 'em so; blow, Tony, blow!
Blow, Tony, blow; O blow, Tony; blow, Tony; blow, Tony, blow![12]

After the rice was separated from the stalk, the rice was put into a large fanner, which was a coiled basket (like a sweetgrass basket) that was used to throw the rice up into the air to get the wind to blow away the chaff.[13] Although it is often said that rice was an everyday menu item, in the days of slavery and post-emancipation, rice was not necessarily eaten every day because people grew their own rice. It was harvested and cleaned on Saturday and then cooked on Sunday.[14]

Rice cultivation, as mentioned, was incredibly difficult work. One Captain Basil Hall, a British naval officer, traveler and author of the early 1800s, wrote that it was

> the most unhealthy work in which the slaves were employed, and that in spite of every care, they sank under it in great numbers. The causes of this dreadful mortality are the constant moisture and heat of the atmosphere, together with the alternating flooding and drying of the fields on which the Negroes [sic] are perpetually at work, often ankle deep in mud, with their bare heads exposed to the fierce rays of the sun.[15]

One common dish that is still served throughout the Lowcountry and southern states is red rice, which is an important dish in Gullah Geechee culture to this day. Some say it is an adaptation of jollof, a West African one-pot dish named after the Wolof people of Senegal and Gambia[16] that incorporates rice with tomatoes, assorted spices and different types of vegetables, meats and/or seafood (depending on who is making it). There are others who say that red rice is a reworking of thieboudienne, a one-pot rice dish that incorporates tomatoes with fish and vegetables and is the national dish of Senegal.[17]

Music

Spirituals, hymns and shouts were all types of singing done by enslaved West Africans. Many of these are preserved and showcased in contemporary performances. Characteristics of spirituals include swaying bodies, clapping hands, tapping feet, solo leads and choral repetitions.[18] One type of singing of enslaved Africans was the "call and response" style, which is usually when groups or individuals sing or shout out a phrase or question (the call) and others in the performance answer (the response).[19] In a religious setting, it is sometimes thought of as a spiritual. In a work or labor setting, it was used to help set the pace of work.

One major component to the evolution of enslaved Africans' music was the denial of the use of drums by the plantation masters. Drums were thought to be a way to secretly communicate messages among the slaves to

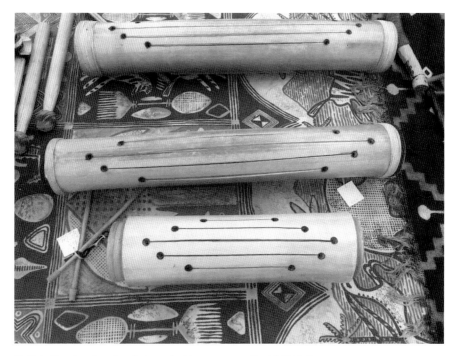

Gullah Geechee handcrafted musical instruments. *Patrick Holladay*.

pass information or to plan escapes. The Gullah Geechee people, however, adapted and used other means of rhythm like clapping and pounding the ground with stout sticks. The enslaved people also used tools on hand like washboards, metal buckets and the ends of hoes to keep rhythm. Gullah Geechee folks also kept rhythm with their hands and feet on the floors of praise houses; these were usually polyrhythmic—two or more different rhythms at the same time—patterns and frequently used in praise and dance.[20] In modern music, the slave songs, ring shouts, work songs and spirituals (including polyrhythm) can all be seen to have influenced blues, gospel, jazz and many other musical genres.

One example of a very well-known Gullah Geechee song is "Kumbaya." This is the song that was sung during 1960s protests and for decades around campfires at youth camps of all sorts. But the reality is that it was not designed for those things. It is a spiritual song. The title "Kumbaya" was likely an outgrowth of the misunderstanding of the Gullah Geechee pronunciation of "come by here."[21] The song is not about wholesome, friendly hand-holding in front of a flickering campfire. The song is prayer to God to "come," to help, to heal, to be present in times of difficulty. "Kum ba ya my Lord, kum ba ya. Kum ba ya my Lord, kum ba ya…Someone's crying, Lord, kum ba ya. Someone's crying, Lord, kum ba ya." Thankfully, in 2017, Representative Buddy Carter of Georgia stood in Congress and officially recognized "Kumbaya" and the Gullah Geechee people as the originators of the song.[22]

Spirituality

Along with music comes spirituality, and in Gullah Geechee culture, the two are deeply intertwined. Ring shouts are traditional spirituals that took place during prayer meetings and times of worship. The "ring" refers to a counterclockwise circular movement of the line of people in the ring shout. This movement comes from a West African tradition of moving in such a manner as they addressed their gods and ancestors in an ever-quickening movement and tempo.[23]

The "shout" is the loud prayer and singing that came along with the counterclockwise movement. The "shout is a call and response style of singing with shouters moving around the circle with a shuffling movement that keep the feet firmly connected to the ground at all times."[24] The evolution of the shout in Gullah Geechee culture comes from the addition of beliefs from Christianity.[25]

Geechee Gullah ring shouters group at Fort Frederica National Monument. *Patrick Holladay*.

Closely tied to these ring shout experiences was the praise house.[26] The praise house was generally a small building used for worship that was built on a plantation; a number still exist and are the focus of preservation efforts.[27] In the praise house, the members of the body would either be active participants or watch the ring shout.[28] New members to the congregation were often asked to lead the ring shout to exhibit their skills as a way to welcome them to the praise house worship.

One other important aspect of religion and spirituality was the numerous baptisms in streams, creeks, ponds and tidal areas around Gullah Geechee communities. As Gullah Geechee people lived in coastal and island environments, the use of the tidal creeks and ocean corresponded with the daily low and high tides. The tradition was such that baptisms were conducted at high tide so that when low tide occurred, all the baptized person's sins and transgressions were pulled away into the ocean as the water retreated.

Language

The Gullah Geechee language stems from an oral culture, without any written language until sometime in the 1900s. The language was based on proverbs, storytelling, songs and passing memories from one generation to the next. Of particular importance were the *griots*, who were caretakers of oral traditions and functioned as historians, storytellers, poets, genealogists and musicians.[29] These West African "bards" told the stories and performed the songs regularly for the community and were responsible for passing this knowledge to the younger generations, who then became the keepers of the culture. This knowledge extended to family lines, trades, foodways, traditions and life skills, among others.

Gullah Geechee people developed a separate Creole (or pidgin) language that is the only African American Creole language in the United States. Some interesting examples of West African and Gullah Geechee words are present in today's American English. For example, the West African word for okra is *tshingombo* (gumbo), which should be familiar. *Nguba* (goober) is peanut, *kuta* (cooter) is turtle and *yam* is sweet potato. Some terms that are found in Gullah Geechee only are *buckruh* or *buckra*, which means the one who governs and is used as a term for white man. *Dayclean* is dawn, and *adunu* means to be away. There are also frequently used sayings or proverbs like "*mus tek cyear a de root fa headle tre,*" which means "you need to take care of the root in order to heal the tree." Another is *"Mary's foot is break,"* which means "Mary is pregnant."

There is some discussion, in terms of language, that Gullah is spoken in the Carolinas and Geechee in Georgia[30] or that Geechee is a sub-dialect of Gullah. But the Gullah Geechee language in itself is an amalgam, and many Gullah Geechee will include all the language as one mother tongue with many dialects arising from which state, island or even individual community you were raised in. There is also some discussion that in Georgia there were saltwater Geechee (those who lived on the island) and freshwater Geechee (who lived inland), and each had a distinct dialect.

Gullah Wars (or Seminole Wars)

As slavery was illegal in the Spanish colony of Florida, many enslaved Africans fled to freedom there. When they arrived, they established "maroon colonies" and frequently intermingled with Native Americans of the area. Maroon colonies were settlements established by runaway slaves, which sometimes also included freed slaves and poor whites, and were formed as a defense against violence toward blacks.[31] Over time, the intermarriage between Native Americans and escaped Gullah Geechee people gave rise to the Black Seminoles.[32]

Maroon colonies were generally in swamplands that were dense and difficult to navigate, had Native American allies and were composed mainly of men, but some had a few women and children.[33] History books will often teach about the Seminole Wars, but seldom part of that history is the inclusion of the Gullah Geechee as a component of the Seminole Indians. The First Seminole War was referred to by General Andrew Jackson as the "Indian and Negro War."[34] It was President Andrew Jackson, in the 1930s, who signed the orders to have the Seminoles forcibly moved to Oklahoma in what became the Second Seminole War.[35] This six-year guerrilla war was a ferocious campaign by the Black Seminoles, which led the commander of the American forces to write to the U.S. War Department, "This, you may be assured, is a negro and not an Indian war."[36]

The Black Seminole (Gullah Geechee) fighters ultimately were overwhelmed in 1842 and sent to the Indian Territory of Oklahoma; the U.S. Army would not send them back to their plantations for fear that their war experiences would cause them to start battles throughout the South in revolt.[37] Once in Oklahoma, however, many escaped to Mexico, established new homes and began to wage war (and protect themselves) against Texas Rangers and Comanche and Apache Indians. After the Civil War, the U.S. Cavalry invited many of the Black Seminoles of Mexico to join their forces, and they became the Seminole Negro Indian Scouts.[38]

Gullah Geechee Cultural Heritage Corridor

The Gullah Geechee Cultural Heritage Corridor was designated by an act of Congress on October 12, 2006, and is laid out in Public Law 109-338. After Congress passed the act, the Gullah Geechee Cultural Heritage Area was created as part of the National Heritage Areas Act of 2006. A national heritage area is a bit different from something like a national park or national battlefield and is not part of the national park system. That said, a national heritage area can receive technical and financial assistance from the National Park Service under the Department of the Interior guidelines.

The Gullah Geechee Cultural Heritage Corridor is tasked with "Telling We Story," or the story of the Gullah Geechee. This includes foodways, music, language, oral traditions, religion, celebrations and heritage. There is a major focus on education, economic development and documentation and preservation. According to Public Law 109-338, the purposes of the corridor are to "recognize the important contributions made to American culture and history by African Americans known as the Gullah/Geechee who settled in the coastal counties of South Carolina, Georgia, North Carolina, and Florida; assist State and local governments and public and private entities in South Carolina, Georgia, North Carolina, and Florida in interpreting the story of the Gullah/Geechee and preserving Gullah/Geechee folklore, arts, crafts, and music; and assist in identifying and preserving sites, historical data, artifacts, and objects associated with the Gullah/Geechee for the benefit and education of the public."[39]

The corridor's vision statement is that it is "an environment that celebrates the legacy and continuing contributions of Gullah Geechee people to our American heritage." The mission of the corridor is to nurture pride and facilitate an understanding and awareness of the significance of "Gullah Geechee history and culture within Gullah Geechee communities; to sustain and preserve land, language, and cultural assets within the coastal communities of South Carolina, Georgia, North Carolina, and Florida; to promote economic development among Gullah

Gullah Geechee Cultural Heritage Corridor information tent at Fort Frederica National Monument. *Patrick Holladay.*

Geechee people; and to educate the public on the value and importance of Gullah Geechee culture."[40]

On January 16, 1865, General William Tecumseh Sherman, on his infamous March to the Sea, issued Special Field Orders No. 15, in which he stated, "The islands from Charleston south, the abandoned rice fields along the rivers for thirty miles back from the sea, and the country bordering the St. John's River, Florida, are reserved and set apart for the settlement of the negroes now made free by the acts of war and the proclamation of the President of the United States."[41] It is from this order that the phrase "forty acres and a mule" came. Each emancipated family in the region was given forty acres of land and an army surplus mule if one was available. In 2006, when the Gullah Geechee Cultural Heritage Corridor was drawn, the land designated in Special Field Orders No. 15 was used to draw the corridor boundaries. There are somewhere around 200,000 Gullah Geechee people living within the corridor.[42]

THE GOLDEN ISLES OF GEORGIA

The paradise of the Golden Isles is located in Glynn County, Georgia. Glynn County is situated along Interstate 95 about halfway between Savannah, Georgia, to the north and Jacksonville, Florida, to the south. It is a mosaic of coastal mainland, four barrier islands, marshlands, rivers, creeks and sandy beaches. Glynn County's constituents are the naturally beautiful Jekyll Island, which is the southernmost island; the picturesque tourist destination of St. Simons Island, slightly north of Jekyll Island; Sea Island, a private luxury resort; Little St. Simons Island, another private island rich in natural resources; and historic Brunswick, the important port city. Beyond historic Brunswick lies the rest of Glynn County, which has its own treasures to find. Outside the old courthouse in Historic Downtown Brunswick is a historic marker that states:

> *Glynn County, one of the eight original Counties of Georgia, was organized under the 1777 Constitution of the State of Georgia. It was named in honor of John Glynn, a member of the British House of Commons who defended the cause of the American Colonies in the difficulties which led to the Revolutionary War. Glynn County contains the lands formerly included in the Colonial Parishes of St. David, St. Patrick, and St. James, which had been organized in 1785. Among the early officials were the Hon. George Walton, Signer of the Declaration of Independence, Judge of the Superior Court; James Spalding, Alexander Bissett, Richard Leake, and Raymond Demere, Justices of the Inferior Court; John Goode, Clerk of the Inferior and Superior Courts; John Palmer, Sheriff; John Burnett, Register of Probates; Richard Bradley, Tax Collector; Martin Palmer, Tax Receiver; Joshua Miller, Surveyor; Jacob Helvestine, Coroner; George Handley (who in 1788 was elected Governor of the State of Georgia) and Christopher Hillary, Legislators; George Purvis, Richard Pritchard, Moses Burnett, John Piles, and John Burnett, Commissioners of Glynn Academy. 063-21 GEORGIA HISTORICAL COMMISSION 1957*

This area became known as the *Golden Isles* because of American poet Sidney Lanier's work titled "The Marshes of Glynn." In that poem, Lanier used the imagery of the sunlight glinting off the bright marsh grass that bespoke of "gold" and the marshes' isles. When Lanier was visiting his wife's brother, Henry C. Day, a resident of Brunswick, in the 1870s, he sat under an oak tree (located in the median on U.S. Highway 17) and wrote the poem.

If you look to your left while traveling south on U.S. Highway 17, shortly before you reach the Gloucester Street turn that takes you into Historic Downtown Brunswick, there is a historic marker that reads:

> LANIER'S OAK—*During his visits to Brunswick in the 1870's Sidney Lanier, Georgia's greatest poet, frequently sat beneath this live oak tree and looked out over "a world of marsh that borders a world of sea." Here he received the inspiration which resulted in some of his finest poems. Of these the best known is "*THE MARSHES OF GLYNN.*" 063-10* GEORGIA HISTORICAL COMMISSION *1956*

The Golden Isles is a wonderful place to live. It is probably one of the most beautiful sites in the whole country, especially with swinging Spanish moss in the live oak trees. It is almost like it is dancing. It is a place of nature, coastal areas, barrier islands, beauty, seclusion and uniqueness. An old saying is that once you get the sand of the Golden Isles in your shoes, you'll always want to come back. It is a place of simple pleasures and a relaxed lifestyle. It a place of sharing voices, engaging stories, families, tradition, laughter and sharing cultures.

Glynn County is a booming tourist destination, receiving over 2.5 million visitors a year that generate about $1 billion in tourism revenue for the area. Georgia itself relies on tourism as its second biggest industry after agriculture. An important component of Georgia's current visitation is from African Americans, who more than double the national average at 27 percent of the total tourist numbers compared to 11 percent in the rest of the United States. Georgia is also the number-one state for African American family reunions.

The interest in Georgia's African American and Gullah Geechee traditions is becoming increasingly important. In the first half of the twentieth century, there was a dramatic rate of change for racial composition in the southern coastal areas and barrier islands. The ratio of black to white population in the coastal South, which had been three to one in 1850, declined to two to one in 1900 and to one-half to one in 1950. The white population of Georgia began to grow bigger than the African American population all the way back to the 1930s.[43]

The Golden Isles has lost an enormous part of its traditional Gullah Geechee culture with the invasion of tourism and resorts. Resorts, golf courses and coastal suburban development on the islands led to steadily increasing property values and skyrocketing taxes. Island economies have changed from subsistence living to a service-based economy with the increasing numbers of resorts, hotels, restaurants and other ancillary tourism industries. In many cases, these types of jobs do not pay enough for people who have lived on the islands for generations to be able to pay their property taxes (because hotels, resorts and second homes drive up property values). Many islanders have been forced to leave their homes because of the escalating taxes caused by development and population growth.[44] This loss of land creates a strong challenge for Gullah Geechee leaders and elders in the preservation of their culture and heritage.[45]

Yet in the face of these challenges and difficulties, there are individuals and organizations that strive to continue their culture in the Golden Isles. One of those groups is the St. Simons African American Heritage Coalition (see part II for more on this nonprofit organization). For over forty years, the St. Simons African American Heritage Coalition has held its annual Georgia Sea Islands Festival on the first Saturday of June to celebrate Gullah Geechee culture of the Golden Isles and beyond. The festival celebrates the Gullah Geechee musical traditions, crafts and food of the coastal barrier islands. Smoked mullet, fried fish, sweet potato pone, homemade ice cream

Georgia Sea Islands Festival on St. Simons Island. *Patrick Holladay.*

and demonstrations of traditional Gullah Geechee knitting, cast nets and sweetgrass baskets attract visitors from all over the country and abroad.

Each year, the highlight of the Georgia Sea Islands Festival is the musicians who perform spirituals, work songs and other traditions handed down by their ancestors. It is a true and proud long-running tradition celebrating the Gullah Geechee people. Emory Rooks, a festival organizer and leader in the St. Simons African American Heritage Coalition, was quoted as saying, "This is a way to celebrate African-Americans and the Gullah Geechee heritage through our food, dancing, entertainment, and arts and crafts."[46]

The festival on St. Simons Island was first organized in 1977 by members of the Georgia Sea Island Singers, Mable Hillery and Bessie Jones. It was later carried on by Frankie Quimby, also of the Georgia Sea Island Singers, and (as was mentioned) is continued today by the St. Simons African American Heritage Coalition. The connection between the Georgia Sea Island Singers and the Georgia Sea Islands Festival is profoundly important. Both the singing group and the festival have been instrumental in the preservation and continuation of Gullah Geechee heritage in the Golden Isles. One of the leaders of both initiatives was Bessie Jones.

Bessie Jones was the charismatic singer most often associated with the Georgia Sea Island Singers among all the group's members. She was born in 1902 and spent her youth in Dawson, Georgia. She moved to St. Simons Island in 1919. At the time, she was invited to sing with Spiritual Singers Society of Coastal Georgia, which she did for many years. Part of that success also led to a short solo career and a performance at the famed Carnegie Hall with the support of Pete Seeger, the acclaimed folk singer. Her solo albums include *So Glad I'm Here* (1973) and *Step It Down* (1975).

Bessie learned many songs from her grandparents that were well over 100 years old. Her grandfather Jet Sampson had been enslaved from West Africa in 1843, yet he lived to 105 years old and was key in passing down the memories of both slavery and West African traditions. In 1982, Bessie was the recipient of a National Heritage Fellowship from the National Endowment for the Arts. Bessie passed away in 1984 and is buried in Union Cemetery on St. Simons Island (see part II).

The Georgia Sea Island Singers arose from the tradition of song that has permeated the Sea Islands since West Africans were enslaved and brought to the region. There is a relatively good history and documentation of the songs the Georgia Sea Island Singers performed since the early 1900s. Back in 1924, Lydia Parrish—who had built trust with the locals by spending many winters on St. Simons Island with her husband, Maxfield Parrish[47]—

helped organize the Spiritual Singers Society of Coastal Georgia. She was instrumental in helping the singers perform at venues like the Cloister Hotel on neighboring Sea Island and the Parrishes' home on St. Simons. Her collections of songs that she curated from locals was first published in 1942 as *Slave Songs of the Georgia Sea Islands.*

In the 1930s, performances were held at the Sea Island Casino, where Lorenzo Dow Turner (well known for being the first academic linguist to study Gullah Geechee language) made recordings of the singing. It was at this time that Bessie Jones, the famed singer, joined the Spiritual Singers Society of Coastal Georgia.[48] Shortly after that, in 1935, Alan Lomax, the legendary collector of folk songs,[49] made his recordings of the Spiritual Singers Society on St. Simons Island. Lomax returned in the 1950s to make more recordings, which are believed to have been made at the Historic Harrington School (see part II). The group was formally organized as the Georgia Sea Island Singers in 1963 and comprised John Davis, Peter Davis, Emma Lee Ramsey, Bessie Jones and Mable Hillery. They were again recorded by Alan Lomax in New York City in 1965. Another notable performance was at the 1976 inauguration ceremony for President Jimmy Carter, who was a native Georgian. Later members of the Georgia Sea Island Singers were Frankie Quimby (who led the group after 1984), Douglas Quimby, Tony Merrell, Joangela Jones Stephens and members of Bessie Jones's family.

Another very well-known person who was born and raised on St. Simons Island is the National Football League legend Jim Brown. He was born in 1936 on the island to the professional boxer Swinton Brown and his wife, Theresa.[50] Swinton Brown, however, wasn't in Jim's life for long. Shortly after Jim's birth, he left his family forever, and Jim was subsequently left with his great-grandmother and grandmother to raise when his mother moved to Long Island, New York, to find work.[51] When he was eight years old, Jim moved to Long Island to rejoin his mother. He later recollected about his time growing up on St. Simons Island:

> *When I was growing up in Georgia, I guess we were supposed to be poor… but we weren't poor. We had all the crab and fish and vegetables that we could eat. The house was so small and weather-beaten, but I lived well. Because there was so much family there, a whole community of people who cared about each other. See, that was my foundation. I'd hate to have to come up without that.*[52]

Jim Brown, NFL legend, on St. Simons Island, age fifteen. *Tyler Bagwell.*

Jim Brown went on to a successful college football career at Syracuse University, where he was a Heisman Trophy contender. He went on to an all-time great professional football career with the Cleveland Browns, led the league in rushing for eight years, made the Pro Bowl every year of his career and won the NFL Championship in 1964 before he retired in 1966 after a nine-year career.[53] He then went on to have a diverse film and television acting career that included iconic movies like *The Dirty Dozen* and *The Running Man* with Arnold Schwarzenegger. But Brown was no stranger to the island over the course of his life. In an interview in 2014, he said of St. Simons Island, "This is home. I love it here.... Through my younger years I came back pretty much every year, this island is a unique place....We just enjoyed the nature. I was an island child. That was in my blood."[54]

Finally, there is Amy Roberts. Not only a coauthor of this book, she is also considered by many to be the matriarch of the Golden Isles and keeper of this place's history and culture. Amy's reflection on growing up in the Golden Isles:

> *I was born in the Golden Isles on St. Simons Island, Georgia. I played in the only park on St. Simons Island for African Americans called Demere Park (which is still a park on Demere Road). I had daycare at the Jackson home with lunch provided, which was a great tuna fish sandwich and soup. I attended the Harrington Graded School, as it was known then. But all the schools in the county for African Americans were closed when I was an elementary student, and we were bused to Brunswick, Georgia. At the time, St. Simons Elementary School had been built, but African Americans were not allowed to attend there.*
>
> *St. Simons was very quiet. Back then, Demere Road was paved, but the other streets were still dirt. The families all traveled around by walking, bikes or driving. At the Village Pier area, we would go to the Community Market for food and St. Simons Drug Store for medicine. And the dress shop for clothes, but of course, we had to put clothes on layaway. People would go fishing and crabbing all day. After a day of fishing and crabbing, clean air was a plus. We slept good at night.*
>
> *The neighbors were happy, with children playing together. All the children that I grew up with, we are still friends. As children, we played all over the neighborhood visiting all the African American families. Some families made good peanut butter and jelly sandwiches for lunch. Children would go to the park to do homework and afterschool activities like basketball,*

softball, jacks, checkers and card games. The island was very clean, with children to help keep the area clean.

You could see beautiful butterflies and birds all over the place. There was very little crime. In the African American community, you could walk down the street and leave your door open and no one would enter your home. On the causeway (F.J. Torras Causeway today), there were beautiful plants on the side of the road bed (yellow, white and pink). What a lovely sight riding on the causeway.

Black and white relationships on St. Simons Island was not a real problem because we respect each other. A lot of black entertainers came to the Golden Isles with Chic Morrison (local man). He played with a big band that traveled to this area. Yes, they played at the juke joints for African Americans on St. Simons Island. In the time period of 1930 to 1950, the juke joints were Atlantic Inn, Melody Lounge and Blue Inn. These places had shutters for windows.

Lastly, the African American churches played a very important part in our lives. All of the African American churches had a closeness. We would travel to other churches in the Golden Isles to help them celebrate. The beautiful moss-covered oak trees and canopy of leaves that we drove under…the breeze was cool. What a beautiful childhood it was for me. I thank my elders for giving me the warmth of a village.

PART II

St. Simons Island

The western colonial beginnings of St. Simons, which are intricately tied to the island's embroilment in West African enslavement and the roots of the Gullah Geechee people, started with General James Edward Oglethorpe, the British soldier who founded Georgia and became its first governor. On St. Simons Island, he established a defensive fort, which he named Frederica after Frederick, the Prince of Wales. The main reason for its construction was as a headquarters as a command post in the conflict with Spanish troops for control of the region. There is more about Fort Frederica later in this chapter.

There are three historic African American neighborhoods on St. Simons Island that were settled by emancipated slaves following the Civil War. These are South End, Harrington and Jewtown. Jewtown was named for the general store built by Sig Levinson and his son, Robert. The Levinson family tried to get locals to call their settlement "Levinsonton," but people used "Jewtown" instead, and the name persists to this day (the store closed in 1921).[55] Notable areas discussed in this chapter are found in all three historic neighborhoods. In South End are Emanuel Baptist Church, remembrances of Neptune Small and Hazel's Café. The Historic Harrington School is in the Harrington community, with the First African Baptist Church a short drive north of there and Gould Cemetery slightly south. St. Ignatius Church, St. Paul Baptist Church and Union (Strangers) Cemetery are all found in Jewtown.

The Abbott Obelisk at Fort Frederica National Monument

No greater glory, no greater honor, is the lot of man departing than a feeling possessed deep in his heart that the world is a better place for his having lived.
—*Robert S. Abbott*

Fort Frederica National Monument, with the Robert Abbott obelisk and the bust to memorialize Robert Abbott and his newsboys, is located at 6515 Frederica Road. Robert Sengstacke Abbott was born on St. Simons Island as the descendant of former enslaved West Africans. He was a bright and driven young man who learned trades like printmaking as he grew up. Robert's father died at an early age, so that left just Robert and his mother and cousins, although his mother did remarry. The family had a large property near the First African Baptist Church on Frederica Road, which was part of an old Oglethorpe plantation.

Robert Abbott and his ancestry were connected to the Stevens plantation or what was also known as the Oatlands Plantation, owned by a Captain Charles Stevens.[56] Charles Stevens was an immigrant from Denmark who settled on St. Simons Island in the early 1840s.[57] The Oatlands Plantation, known for growing rice, cotton and cane, changed hand many times. It was started by James Bruce in the late 1770s, and after Charles Stevens, it was acquired by John Couper, who had interests in the Cannon's Point Plantation and the Hamilton Plantation on St. Simons Island. Part of the Oatlands Plantation is where Fort Frederica National Monument now stands.

Robert Abbott's mother started working in German Village with white settlers; the original name of German Village came from a group of immigrants from Salzburg, Germany, whom General James Oglethorpe brought to St. Simons Island to help grow food for Fort Frederica. German Village is next to Musgrove Plantation, which was named for Mary Musgrove, a local woman of mixed Muscogee Creek and English ancestry who spoke English and helped General Oglethorpe negotiate with the local Creek natives. As reward for her assistance, General Oglethorpe gave her five hundred acres of land in this location on St. Simons Island. Near where the village used to stand is a historic marker that reads:

Here in 1736, Oglethorpe settled a group of German Lutherans, known as Salzburgers, and their settlement was called the German Village. These

St. Simons Island

Salzburgers made their living by planting, fishing, and selling their products to the Frederica settlers. When Oglethorpe's regiment was disbanded in 1749 the Salzburgers left St. Simons Island. During the Plantation Era, the Wylly family lived here, their plantation being called "The Village."

Robert Abbott's mother worked at the store in German Village for a married couple with the last name Sengstacke who owned the establishment. This couple had a son named John Sengstacke who was in Germany going to school. When he graduated, he came to St. Simons Island to be with his family. Wouldn't you believe that a love affair came about? John Sengstacke married Robert's mother, Flora Butler Abbott, and he became a mentor to Robert Abbott. John Sengstacke was also in the printing business, and this is where Robert first began to learn about printing.

Robert Abbott wanted a full and enriching schooling, so he was educated first at the Beach Institute in Savannah. Following that, he went on to earn a degree in printing from Hampton Institute, a historically black university in Virginia. When he graduated, he went to Chicago with about twenty-two cents in his pocket. It was there that Robert earned a law degree from the Kent College of Law in Chicago in 1898. Due to the times and a widespread prevalence of discrimination in the field of law, Robert found that this was a very difficult career path to follow. He made the decision to turn to journalism and was the founder, editor and publisher of the *Chicago Defender* newspaper. He moved his mother and stepfather up to Chicago with him, and they all worked together. His stepfather helped him and taught him more of the printing trade to help get the newspaper started.

The *Chicago Defender* was established in 1905 and was published for an African American readership. The paper was unique in its stance for social justice and equality for blacks and its strong renunciation of violence against blacks, particularly lynching, during this Jim Crow era when the southern states enforced racial segregation. The paper drew strength from its conviction and also its journalists, some of whom were quite famous, like Langston Hughes, the poet and novelist.

Copies of the *Chicago Defender* were passed around from person to person and read out loud to people in churches and other community spaces. There have been estimates, based on the idea that the paper was read aloud to groups, that although weekly sales were around 100,000, as many as 500,000 got the news from the *Defender* each week. Robert Abbott became one of the country's first African American millionaires in the 1920s on the strength of his newspaper.

Robert S. Abbott Obelisk at Fort
Frederica National Monument.
*Georgia Department of Economic
Development.*

After founding the *Defender*, Robert Abbott found help in distributing his newspaper throughout the South, where it was illegal. The Pullman Porters, men who worked on trains, under the direction of A. Philip Randolph, the founder of the Pullman Porters,[58] put his newspapers in their mail bags to be distributed throughout the South. The porters would sling bags of newspapers off the train at predetermined sites where local African American men would grab them and hide them in the trunks of their cars before distributing them among the community.

Abbott's newspaper's descriptions of opportunities and improved quality of life for African Americans in the North and Midwest of the United States were instrumental in the "Great Migration," the exodus from the South to the Northeast, Midwest and West Coast. More than six million African Americans moved between 1915 and 1970, with many ending their journeys in places like New York, Chicago, Detroit and Cleveland.[59]

Abbott had the obelisk that is found at Fort Frederica made in Savannah, Georgia, in 1938. He had it brought to St. Simons Island and erected on the land that eventually became Fort Frederica. He selected that site because that area is supposed to be a cemetery connected to the plantation that was there. In fact, Fort Frederica staff are doing some research to see if it is a cemetery. There is a potential that Robert Abbott's relatives (including his father) could be buried there. The obelisk is dedicated to members of his family, including Thomas Abbott (father), Gelia Abbott (aunt) and Mary Abbott Finnick (aunt).

Fort Frederica National Monument is run by the National Park Service and is free to visit, with extensive grounds to tour, a visitors' center and an educational theater. It is open every day from 9:00 a.m.to 5:00 p.m. and only closed on Thanksgiving, Christmas Day and New Year's Day. Just inside the grounds of the fort is a plaque on the ground that gives this brief history:

In 1736, on this historic site, Fort Frederica was constructed by the early settlers of the Colony of Georgia under General James Edward Oglethorpe. It was the strongest fortification built by Great Britain on American soil and its purpose was to protect Georgia and the colonies to the north from the Spaniards who were already established in Florida. In 1742, six years later, more than 3,000 Spanish troops landed in 52 vessels at Gascoigne Bluff on St. Simons island. The British forces advanced to meet them and decisively defeated the Spaniards in the Battle of Bloody Marsh. Thus Fort Frederica fulfilled the purpose for which it was built and Georgia remained a British colony. In 1903 after more than a century and a half of disuse and decay the small remaining ruins were conveyed from Mrs. Belle Stevens Taylor to Mrs. Georgia Pace King Wilder as president of the Georgia Society of Colonial Dames of America, who sought to preserve and restore Fort Frederica. In this patriotic undertaking they were assisted by generous citizens of Georgia and other states who formed the Fort Frederica Association and rendered aid in money, property, and services to make this land available for restoration. In 1945 their efforts were rewarded when the United States Government established Fort Frederica National Monument.

After Robert made his fortune, he helped the slave-owning family that had formerly owned his ancestors and sent two of their children to college. The situation turned all the way around from being a slave to being a supporter. The families were actually a close group. Inside the Fort Frederica visitors' center is a ceramic bust of Robert Abbott and the Newsboys. The Newsboys were the children who carried the newspapers and sold them on the streets. Abbott was a music lover and taught some of the Newsboys to sing and play instruments. They eventually formed a Newsboys Band. Lionel Hampton was one of the Newsboys who went on to an incredibly successful music career, performing with many other great artists and earning numerous distinguished awards.[60]

The Historic Harrington School

The Historic Harrington School is located at 291 South Harrington Road. The Harrington neighborhood was settled by freed slaves after the Civil War. In colonial times, the land was owned by Captain Raymond Demere, who was in the command of General James Oglethorpe, the founder of the British colony of Georgia. The name "Harrington" was in honor of Demere's former commander, a Lord Harrington. Captain Demere built a home here that was called Harrington Hall, and on its approximate location is a marker that reads:

> *Capt. Raymond Demere, a native of France, served many years in the British army at Gibraltar before coming to Georgia in 1738 as an officer in Oglethorpe's Regiment. His home, Harrington Hall, was located at this site. Later generations of Demere family lived at the south end of St. Simons Island where their plantation was called Mulberry Grove*

Following emancipation, the Harrington area was settled by former slaves who were from the more northern part of the island. Over the years, it evolved into its own self-enclosed entity, and by the 1900s, it had not only the Harrington School but also a store, gas station, barbershop, two churches, a restaurant called the Plantation Supper Club and more. The community is laid out like a large H if you were to view it from above. North and South Harrington Roads are parallel to each other and are connected by a short road called Harrington Lane.[61]

The Historic Harrington School Cultural Center, formerly known as the Harrington Graded School, was built in 1924 and served as the main educational structure for three African American communities on St. Simons Island. The land the school was built on was donated by the Whing family, who were residents of the Harrington community. The impetus for the construction of the school likely originated with a July 1919 Glynn County Board of Education decision to go ahead with three Rosenwald schools (schools funded by Sears chairman Julius Rosenwald for rural African American communities). In fact, a 1920 survey of Brunswick and Glynn County schools by the U.S. Bureau of Education recommended that a Rosenwald school or similar plan be built for "colored students" on St. Simons Island.

The name of the school came from the fact that it was built in the Harrington community of the island. The Harrington community was settled by emancipated slaves who had worked on the plantations on St. Simons Island for the Coupers and the Goulds. The Historic Harrington School hosted grades one through seven until desegregation in the 1960s, when students left to attend other schools in Brunswick and St. Simons. In 1968, it was converted to a daycare center and was used for this purpose until 1970. It was largely abandoned after that and sat unused for decades.

Historic Harrington School. *Patrick Holladay.*

To preserve the one-room Historic Harrington School, Isadora Hunter, a lifelong Harrington community resident and member of the Whing family, donated her portion of the heirs' property land to the St. Simons Land Trust and Glynn County in 2004. Since 2004, the St. Simons African American Heritage Coalition, in partnership with the St. Simons Land Trust, has been active in the fundraising, management and operations of the school. Yet it was a long and difficult road to preserve and restore the school. The official lease started in 2011 for ninety-nine years at one dollar per year.

The St. Simons African American Heritage Coalition (SSAAHC) is a 501(c)(3) nonprofit corporation established in 2000. The organization was founded by Mrs. Isadora Hunter and other African American property owners concerned about the rising number of new real estate developments around St. Simons Island. These new developments were invading African American neighborhoods. The rise in property taxes brought on by these new homes, condominiums and retail establishments was forcing many African Americans to sell or abandon their properties. So it became the mission of the SSAAHC to help property owners retain their land and educate other African Americans about the importance of preserving and revitalizing St. Simons Island's African American communities. In the spring of 2002, SSAAHC launched a land retention initiative; owners placed bright yellow signs on their property declaring, "Don't Ask—Won't Sell." A key part of SSAAHC's purpose has been to teach the area young people about their rich cultural heritage so that they will learn to take pride in their Gullah Geechee ancestry.

In 2005, a United States National Park Service cultural resource study identified the Harrington School as an important place within the Gullah Geechee Cultural Heritage Corridor. In 2009, the Georgia Trust for Historic Preservation placed the school on its "Places in Peril" list. Although it was originally slated for demolition, in 2010, a three-phase restoration program with a capital campaign of over $300,000 began, and the school was rescued and restored. It officially reopened with a ribbon cutting in August 2017. The goals of the Harrington School are 1) historical preservation and education, 2) heritage and cultural tourism and 3) conservation, to include habitat protection and interpretation.

Over the years, the schoolhouse was much more than just a place to learn. The community gathered here for Halloween apple-bobbing parties in the fall, plays and covered-dish dinners and visits from Santa and Christmas exchanges. In the spring, there were Easter activities, the plaiting of the Maypole, the prom and graduation. Community organizations such as the Harrington Parent-Teacher Association and the Harrington Civic Club also utilized the building for meetings and fundraising events.

Harrington School under restoration. *Benjamin Galland, H20 Creative Group.*

Harrington School interior and monthly speaker. *Patrick Holladay.*

It was a wonderful place to go to school. The teachers were Adrian Johnson and Luetta Johnson, who lived in the South End community on the island (both are buried in the Union Cemetery off Demere Road behind the Georgia Power station). Adrian Henry Johnson was a native of St. Simons Island and had attended Claflin University in Orangeburg, South Carolina. In Orangeburg, he met Miss Luetta Brown, who was a native of Orangeburg, and the two later married. The two were also active in civic and religious activities. Mr. Johnson was a deacon at Emanuel Baptist Church, and Mrs. Johnson was the choir director for the church.

The land where Demere Park (on Demere Road) still stands was donated by Adrian Johnson, and Johnson Road on St. Simons Island was named in his honor. Many of the South End schoolchildren rode with Mr. and Mrs. Johnson to school in their navy blue four-door Dodge sedan for fifty cents a week. Mrs. Johnson would get into the car every morning with her toast and jelly, and Mr. Johnson would roll the big car down the driveway. A former student recalled the car ride:

> I remember the smell of the toast Mrs. Johnson had. I lived near the Johnsons, so my dad let me ride to school with them. Every morning she would get into the car with the most delicious-smelling toast and coffee. No, she did not ever give us any. But I remember Mr. Johnson always telling her to "Hurry up. We're going to be late." On the ride to the school, Mrs. Johnson would sit and talk with the children about things they would want to accomplish that day in school. Of course, the children were not interested in that and only cared about talking about play time!

The Harrington School itself was divided into two rooms. When you first walk in the front door, that was the younger children's classroom, and the older children were in the back. The younger children could not hear the older children talking but could hear Mr. Johnson's voice booming out from the back room. In the front room, Mrs. Johnson encouraged the younger children to sing because she loved music and could play piano quite well. Mrs. Johnson made dittos (paper copies) of items around the school like leaves and acorns for the children. She also had all of the younger children go outside and collect, for example, ten acorns or ten leaves, and that is how they learned to add, subtract and things of that nature.

Every day started with devotion. The children had to find a Bible verse, and the Bible verse had to correspond with the letter of the alphabet that would be used that day. For example, if the letter for the day was A, then

Mr. Adrian Johnson, teacher at Harrington. *1957 Lighthouse Yearbook. Also published in* Glynn County, Georgia *by Benjamin Allen, Arcadia Publishing.*

the Bible verse would start with a word like "Adam." If a younger child did not know a verse, an older child would come to help find one with the letter, and the younger child would learn it for the next day.

After devotion, there was singing and then quiet games and art. Students had a small piece of crayon and a small piece of chalk for their art lessons. There was also reading that started in first grade. After reading was a little science and then math. After math was lunchtime and recess. Students brought a bag lunch except on Fridays, when one of the parents brought hot dogs. The school sold the hot dogs to the schoolchildren to raise funds to work on a playground that was on North Harrington Road near the school. Sometimes the children would walk to that playground, and sometimes they would walk out to the marsh when they had free time. Games they played included duck-duck-goose, ring around the rosy, London Bridge, dodge ball and hopscotch. After lunch were more lessons on reading comprehension. The children would get into groups, and an older child would sit with a younger child and help them learn.

You will notice in the school that one wall (the east wall) has no windows. Various stories abound. Some say it is because the hurricanes came from the east. Others say it kept the sun rising in the east from coming in, which kept the building cooler. And then others will say that the teachers needed a place to hang the blackboards. It is likely that all of these ideas are true.

Concerning the blackboards: one blackboard was lower than the other because that was for the younger children. Sometimes Mrs. Johnson would give them math problems to work at the blackboard. The younger children learned how to write their numbers using chalk. There is also a large potbelly stove in the school. There was no other heat source, and this stove was used to warm the school on cold days. There was a large coal pile behind the school, and the teachers and children would fetch coal from the pile to feed the stove.

The bathrooms (privies) were in the back, with the boys on one side and the girls on the other. There was no indoor plumbing. Girls were strictly forbidden to go onto the boys' side! That was against the rules, and if you were caught, you could get paddled. Mr. Johnson had "Big Boy" (a leather strap) and Mrs. Johnson had "Patty," but Patty was nice and did not come out too often because Mrs. Johnson did not like to paddle children. She was an extraordinarily sweet woman. One former student reminisced, "I remember Mr. Johnson had that leather strap hung up on the wall. You got it for infractions. What infractions? Oh, nothing big. Things like pulling a girl's hair or shooting spitballs. You did not want to get it, however, because if you did, you'd get it again when you got home."

There have been other personal tributes to the Johnsons collected over the years. One reads, "They were my elementary school teachers at Harrington. Mr. and Mrs. Johnson were truly dedicated to building a foundation for all of the students, and as a result, have made the greatest contribution to my educational background."

As was introduced in part I, Lorenzo Dow Turner spent time in the Harrington community. He interviewed a Harrington resident named Belle Murray, who was also a member of the Whing family and a relative of Isadora Hunter, for his study of African dialects. Turner also recorded several songs for Lydia Parrish, who wrote the book *Slave Songs of the Georgia Sea Islands*. The Harrington connection to language and music continues from there.

In 1935, Alan Lomax, along with folklorists Mary Barnicle and Zora Neale Hurston, traveled to St. Simons Island. Alan Lomax was a folklorist himself who learned from his father, John Lomax, another folklorist. Alan Lomax was one of the very first to recognize the value of recording, collecting and preserving African American music. With his aforementioned partners, he made hundreds of recordings on St. Simons Island in 1935; they are now housed in the Library of Congress under the archive name the Lomax, Hurston and Barnicle Expedition.

In 1961, Alan Lomax filmed the original Georgia Sea Island Singers at the camp located between North and South Harrington Roads. These recordings are part of the Library of Congress and Smithsonian Folkways collection. Before that, in 1959, British folk singer Shirley Collins accompanied Alan Lomax on his trip through the South to record traditional folk music. She wrote about their trip in her book *America Over the Water*. In that book, she described meeting and recording John Davis, Bessie Jones and the Georgia Sea Island Singers:

> *The music was superb, the conditions difficult. We were working in the old school house, and Alan said it was worse than recording inside a barrel. For*

Harrington
Community Park.
Patrick Holladay.

two nights we worked there, taking bottles of bourbon and crates of Coca Cola to keep everyone going. The nights were hot and sultry. One night, after we'd opened up the windows to let in some much-needed air, I counted moths that flew in and settled, and gave up at over four hundred.

This is very interesting because it is likely that those 1959 recordings made with the Georgia Sea Island Singers, now housed at the Library of Congress, were made in the Historic Harrington School.

Immediately adjacent to the Historic Harrington School is the Harrington Community Park. The land that it occupies was also donated by Isadora Hunter when she donated the land and the Harrington School. The park has nice walking trails, two ponds, wildlife and an abundance of natural beauty. It was constructed by Glynn County and is a cooperation between the county and the Harrington residents for its upkeep.

IBO LANDING

Ibo Landing is located down Atlantic Avenue off Frederica Road in a small neighborhood, nestled among privately owned homes. There are about three separate properties that could be the original site, and they are all adjacent to one another. No one really knows exactly which property it is.

Alternatively to visiting the property, it can be viewed traveling east on Sea Island Road by looking north across Dunbar Creek when crossing the small bridge that spans the creek.

The Ibo (sometimes Ebo or Igbo) people are one of Africa's largest ethnic groups and hail mainly from Nigeria, although some of the nearly twenty-five million population live in nearby countries.[62] The Ibo Landing site has great significance to many people, including native Africans and clergy of various types from Africa. They have been known to take private tours (with permission) and set up tables with food and ceremonial artifacts. They will get into the water and collect water in small bottles to take home with them. They called it "blessed water." They often think they can feel the spirits.

In the 1930s and 1940s, the older folks called it the end of the world and wouldn't go there. One old-time local fisherman named Enoch Proctor was heard to say, "I'm not going out to fish there because my family say that is the end of the world." They used to go fishing on the boats on the creek. They would anchor and doze off, and when they woke up, the boat would have been moved to another spot. And guess what? At the new spot, they

Ibo Landing view from a tourist trolley. *Patrick Holladay.*

caught a lot of fish. So they believed the spirits had moved them to the new spot to help them. These were the people who used to go fishing on Dunbar River. It is now Dunbar Creek, as it has naturally started getting smaller. Occasionally, you can see bottlenose dolphins swimming by.

Those noble marine mammals are allowed to live freely, but that was not the case for the Ibo people brought to Ibo Landing. In Georgia, slavery had been outlawed and prohibited by the time of this Ibo incident. So unscrupulous slave traders worked in illegal and clandestine ways, slipping ships up creeks and small rivers that crisscrossed the Georgia coast and islands. In 1803, on a small schooner called the *York*, they slinked up Dunbar Creek, which runs through the middle of St. Simons Island, to deposit their cargo of illegally enslaved West African Ibo tribesmen.

Back in West Africa, the Ibo people had walked onto the ship voluntarily because they thought they were coming to be employed by a plantation in America. When they reached the Mid-Atlantic, they were told they were to become slaves and were chained together. They could not accept that, as they had been free at home. The legend says that somewhere around eight to thirteen of the tribesmen deliberately drowned themselves at this spot in Dunbar Creek. They were led by their chieftain while singing an Igbo hymn seeking the protection of the Ibo god known as Chukwu, the supreme god and creator of the world in the Ibo religion.[63] There is an ancient Ibo saying:

Ibo Landing on Dunbar Creek. *Georgia Department of Economic Development.*

"The water brought us here, the water will take us away." The rest became slaves on the plantations on St. Simons Island. This story was believed by many African American locals to be a myth. But in the 1980s—reportedly beginning with the work of H.A. Sieber, a native of North Carolina who lived on St. Simons for a couple of years—evidence began to suggest that all the stories that had been passed down from generation to generation were indeed true.[64]

The actual story of Ibo Landing was solely passed down from generation to generation by oral history. In 1940, the Georgia branch of the Federal Writers' Project visited St. Simons Island and collected many stories, including this one. This collection was later published in the book *Drums and Shadows*, which includes much of the African American and Gullah Geechee folklore of the Georgia coast.

THE LEGACY OF NEPTUNE SMALL

There are two remembrances for Neptune Small in the village area off Mallery Street near the pier and St. Simons Lighthouse. One is a statue in the visitors' center that was cast in bronze by local artist Kevin Pullen. The other is a plaque in the ground across the street from the visitors' center in Neptune Park.

Neptune Small was born in 1831 and was the slave of the King family, who owned Retreat Plantation. The South End of St. Simons Island was historically mostly part of the Retreat Plantation (which is now mostly a golf course). Neptune's main duty as an enslaved man was to look after the King children of Ann Page King and Thomas Butler King. At the onset of the Civil War in 1861, Neptune went with Henry Lord Page King, one of the sons of the family, to fight with the Confederate army and journeyed to Virginia to do so. When Page and Small arrived outside Fredericksburg, Virginia, one account said that Neptune cooked dinner. After they had eaten, while Neptune was cleaning the dishes, King remarked, "Neptune, there's a big fight tomorrow morning and good men will eat their last supper tonight."[65] This is said to have chilled Neptune to his core.

In December 1862, Captain King was killed in the Battle of Fredericksburg in Virginia as he attempted to return from delivering a message to another part of the Confederate army. When Neptune heard of his death, he went onto the violent battlefield at high personal danger

Visitors' center on St. Simons Island. *Patrick Holladay.*

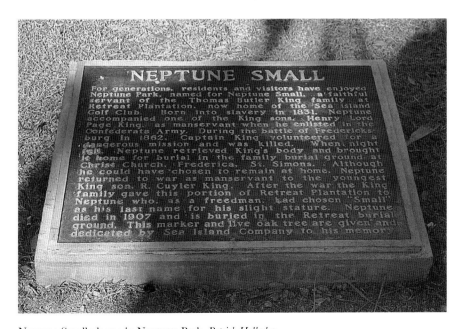

Neptune Small plaque in Neptune Park. *Patrick Holladay.*

Neptune Small. *Coastal Georgia Historical Society.*

to retrieve King's body. He then brought the body back to St. Simons Island, where Captain King was laid to rest at Christ Church Cemetery. After the Civil War, Neptune was given a piece of land owned by the King family. He chose "Small" as his last name because he was short in height. Neptune Small died in August 1907 and is buried in the cemetery on Retreat Plantation that is designated for the plantation's slaves and their descendants. That particular cemetery is now located on the private Sea Island Golf Club and cannot be visited by tourists without special permission to pass through the guard gate.

When you arrive at Neptune Park beside the pier, look for a bronze tablet embedded in the ground that recounts his story. Neptune Park is part of the property that Neptune received from the King family after he received his freedom. The plaque reads:

> *For generations, residents and visitors have enjoyed Neptune Park, Named for Neptune Small, a faithful servant of the Thomas Butler King family at Retreat Plantation, now home of the Sea Island Golf Club. Born into slavery in 1831, Neptune accompanied one of the King's sons, Henry Lord Page King, as manservant when he enlisted in the Confederate Army. During the battle of Fredericksburg in 1862, Captain King volunteered for a dangerous mission and was killed. When night fell, Neptune retrieved King's body and brought it home for burial in the family burial grounds at Christ Church Frederica, St. Simons. Although he could have chosen to remain at home, Neptune returned to war as manservant to the youngest King son R. Cuyler King. After the war the King family gave this portion of Retreat Plantation to*

Neptune Small statue by artist Kevin Pullen. *Patrick Holladay.*

Neptune who as a freedman had chosen Small as his last name for his slight stature. Neptune died in 1907 and is buried in the Retreat burial ground. This marker and live oak tree are given and dedicated by Sea Island Company to his memory.

THE HAMILTON PLANTATION TABBY SLAVE CABINS

The tabby slave cabins are near Gascoigne Bluff on the grounds of the Epworth by the Sea Methodist Center at 100 Arthur J. Moore Drive. The cabins stand on what was Hamilton Plantation, which was a plantation owned by James Hamilton and John Cooper on what is now Gascoigne Bluff Park. James Hamilton and John Cooper turned Hamilton Plantation into a long-staple cotton producer. Hamilton arrived in America from Scotland during the time of the Revolutionary War, when he established a two-story home on the property; in his later years, he moved to Philadelphia, where he died in 1829.[66] A historic marker can be found here that reads:

> In 1774 Major Pierce Butler of South Carolina purchased Hampton Point in northwestern St. Simons Island, and by the 1790s Hampton was developed into the island's largest cotton plantation in land and slave population. Signer of the Constitution and member of the new U.S. Senate, Butler moved from Charleston to Philadelphia. In 1838 Major Butler's grandson, Pierce Butler, and his abolitionist wife, British actress Fanny Kemble, traveled to Georgia to inspect the Butler plantations. She wrote a scathing account that was published during the Civil War, creating much sensation in the North and in England. In 1859, to cover mounting debts, 436 slaves from Butler's Georgia plantations were sold in Savannah, an event known as "The Weeping Time."

Gascoigne Bluff Park has been many things over the years, including a Native American village, a naval station for Captain James Gascoigne in the 1700s and a lumbering operation; live oak trees harvested here were used in the construction of the USS *Constitution*, also known as "Old Ironsides." A lumber mill was established here in 1874 and became a major economic engine and employer with especially good ties to the neighborhood of Jewtown. The lumber mill, called the Dodge-Meigs Company, utilized the old plantation buildings, including the tabby slave cabins, as part of its operation until the last mill was closed in 1903.[67] A concise history is on a marker at the park:

> Throughout the ages Gascoigne Bluff has been the gateway to St. Simons Island. An Indian village was located here. Capt. James Gascoigne of HM Sloop-of-war, HAWK, which convoyed the Frederica settlers on their voyage across the Atlantic in 1736, established headquarters for Georgia's naval forces and had his plantation here. In the invasion of 1742 the Spaniards landed at this Bluff. Live oak timbers for the building of USS CONSTITUTION, better known as "OLD IRONSIDES," and the other vessels of our first US Navy were cut on St. Simons and loaded here in 1794 for shipment North where vessels were built. During the Plantation Era these lands became the sea island cotton plantation of James Hamilton. A wharf here was the shipping center for the St. Simons plantations. 1874–1902 this Bluff was lined with great

Hamilton Plantation sign. *Patrick Holladay*.

mills, where cypress and long leaf yellow pine timbers were sawed into lumber and shipped to all parts of the world. The causeway built in 1924, connecting St. Simons with the mainland, has its terminus here. In 1949 the Methodist Church acquired the upper part of the Bluff and established EPWORTH-BY-THE-SEA as a Conference Center. GHM 063-13 Georgia Historical Commission 1956

The property was then in private residential ownership by Mr. and Mrs. Eugene W. Lewis from Detroit, who had a winter home there until it was purchased in 1949 by the United Methodist Church, which established Epworth by the Sea.[68] Epworth by the Sea is a retreat, conference center, camp, recreation and worship center that was named for John and Charles Wesley's childhood home in Epworth, England.[69] The tranquil grounds of the Epworth by the Sea Methodist Center are freely open to the public and include picnic areas, chapels and a museum. On the Epworth location is a historic marker that encapsulates its history:

In 1945, South Georgia Methodists resolved to establish a religious center. After searching four years for a site, the Sea Island Company offered to sell them 43.53 acres of the Hamilton Plantation. Because the Conference did not have the $40,000, Bishop Arthur J. Moore asked nine laymen to join him in signing a bank note for a tenth of the purchase price. Not one refused. Since D. Abbott Turner never signed a note, he gave $4,000 in cash. Later known as Epworth Pioneers, they were A.J. Strickland, Jr., Alfred W. Jones, Sr., Walter Blasingame, J. Slater Wright, Ben J. Tarbutton, Sr., Leo B. Huckabee, Jerome Crawley, George T. Morris and D. Abbott Turner. On July 25, 1950, in the Wesley tradition, almost 800 Methodists met under moss draped live oaks for the formal opening. Churches and individuals responded, paid the debt and began a tradition of love, prayers and financial support which makes God's ministry at Epworth possible.

The tabby cabins get their name from their composition: tabby. Tabby is a construction material used from the 1500s to the 1800s, made by mixing equal parts lime, water, sand, oyster shells and lime ash (leftover from preparing the lime).[70] Once the tabby mixture was made, it was poured into molds and left to harden; once the forms hardened, they were joined together to make walls and covered with stucco composed of sand and lime.[71] The origin of the word "tabby" is thought to be of African-Arabic origins and means a wall of earth or masonry.[72] Each cabin would have had two rooms and an attic loft for sleeping. It is likely, based on the size and well-constructed buildings, that these cabins were

Cassina Garden Club sign. *Patrick Holladay.*

This page: Tabby cabins. *Patrick Holladay*.

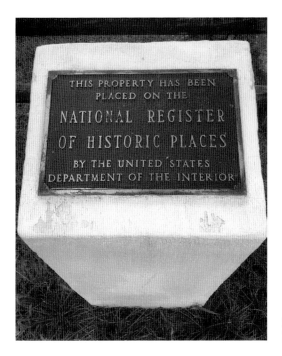

National Register of Historic
Places sign. *Patrick Holladay.*

used by slave families in some position of prominence. Perhaps they were slave foremen among the other slaves.

In 1988, the two cabins were named to the National Register of Historic Places. Look for this plaque at the entrance to the grounds of the cabin. Near the cabins is a historic marker that reads:

> *These houses were slave cabins on the Gascoigne Bluff section of Hamilton Plantation which was developed in 1793 by James Hamilton into one of the largest estates on St. Simons Island. Eventually this Gascoigne Bluff area was given to Glynn County for a park honoring the first naval site in America. These cabins were given to the Cassina Garden Club in 1931 for preservation purposes. ERECTED 1965*

The cabins are easily accessible to visit at any time, but in order to see the interior, an appointment must be made with the Cassina Garden Club, which has been instrumental in the restoration of the cabins and care for the buildings and grounds.

Cemeteries of St. Simons Island

Gould Cemetery

Gould Cemetery is found directly off Frederica Road traveling north and will be seen on the right-hand side of the road. It is directly next door to a golf course and an office building and is wedged between them. The cemetery originated in the 1800s and is managed by First African Baptist Church of St. Simons. There is some evidence that the office building and golf course may be built on some old unmarked graves.[73]

Retreat Cemetery

While this property is the historic burial grounds of all the slaves of Retreat Plantation and their descendants, it is now blocked by a golf course that is in private ownership and only accessible through a security gate with permission. Retreat Plantation was one of the biggest plantations on the South End of St. Simons Island. Although visitors are not allowed to enter the private golf course, there is a historic marker on King's Way slightly north of Frederica Road that reads:

> *In 1804 William Page purchased land on St. Simons Sound and named it Retreat. With later purchases, Retreat became one of the preeminent plantations on St. Simons Island for the production of long-staple cotton. In 1827 the Pages' only child, Anna Matilda, who had married Thomas Butler King of Massachusetts, inherited Retreat. She was active in the management of the plantation and its slave population. Mr. King became a Georgia state senator and U.S. Congressman, where he led efforts to strengthen the U.S. Navy. Retreat land stretched from the Frederica River to the Lighthouse. Part of Retreat, including the Avenue of Oaks, is now home to Sea Island Golf Club, and other portions are residential and commercial areas and public parks. Erected by The Georgia Historical Society, Coastal Georgia Historical Society, Friends of Coastal Georgia History, and Sea Island Company.*

Above: Gould Cemetery sign.
Patrick Holladay.

Right: Retreat Cemetery sign.
*Georgia Department of Economic
Development.*

Union Cemetery (also known as Strangers Cemetery)

The cemetery is located roughly behind Frederica Academy and a Georgia Power station. Following the turn into Frederica Academy, take the immediate turn toward Georgia Power. Then follow the dirt road past the Union/Strangers Cemetery sign. The cemetery is among some trees on the left side of the dirt road. This cemetery was/is for people who were not born on St. Simons Island. If you did not belong to a plantation, you could not be buried in a plantation cemetery. So that is why Union Cemetery was established—for the people who were not born on a plantation. That is why it also has a second name of "Strangers Cemetery," since people not born on St. Simons were, in essence, "strangers." Indeed, these folks did not have any true connection to any plantation where they could be buried in a plantation plot. There's a Gullah Geechee expression of "come yah and been yah." Been yah means *been here*, or those people who were natives and longtime residents. Come yah means *come here* and was the label of people considered newcomers.

Union Memorial Cemetery sign. *Patrick Holladay*.

The cemetery is cared for by Emmanuel Baptist Church and St. Paul Baptist Church. A number of notable island residents have been laid to rest here. These include Jim Brown's aunt, Bessie Jones and Mable Hillery of the Georgia Sea Island Singers, as well as Adrian and Luetta Johnson, the teachers at the Historic Harrington School.

HISTORIC BLACK CHURCHES OF ST. SIMONS ISLAND

First African Baptist Church

First African Baptist Church is located at 5800 Frederica Road. The church was organized in 1859 at Pike's Bluff Plantation, and the Reverend Andrew Neal became the first pastor and served for twenty-eight years. This is the first African American church on St. Simons Island. The Sunday school began in 1875.[74] The impetus for creating this church was that the islanders would have to travel by rowboat to worship at the First African

First African Baptist Church. *Patrick Holladay*.

Baptist Church in Brunswick. Over the years, this became something of a burden and was tiring, so a few of the folks from St. Simons got together and organized the First African Baptist Church on St. Simons.

First African Baptist Church would come to have the first female pastor on the island. The church has been important to the community throughout its history. When it had its anniversary every year, everyone would go on a Thursday night (from the other churches on the island as well). That is because that is when the men had off from work on Sea Island, and the men were the deacons of the church.

St. Ignatius

St. Ignatius is located at 2906 Demere Road. Keep a sharp eye open because it is a very small church by most standards and can be missed. St. Ignatius is a chapel of Christ Church Frederica, which itself was built in 1820 but was mostly destroyed during the Civil War and rebuilt as it stands now in 1884.[75] Christ Church Frederica was established and constructed under the direction of Reverend Anson Greene Phelps Dodge. Christ Church Frederica follows the Methodist tradition, as the brothers John and Charles Wesley, the founders of Methodism, first accompanied General James Oglethorpe to the island to preach. Found beside the entrance to the grounds of Christ Church Frederica is a historic marker that reads:

> *This congregation was established as a mission of the Church of England in February, 1736. The Rev. Charles Wesley, ordained priest of that Church, conducted the first services in the chapel within the walls of Fort Frederica. The Rev. John Wesley, Rector of Christ Episcopal Church, Savannah, also served this mission. Under the name St. James, this was one of the eight original parishes established in 1758. After the Revolution, this and other churches which had been served continuously by clergymen of the Church of England formed the Protestant Episcopal Church in the United States of America. Christ Church was incorporated by the State legislature in 1808 and given a glebe of 108 acres; and in 1823 was one of the three parishes organizing the diocese of Georgia. The first Church built on this property in 1820 was almost destroyed during the War Between the States. The present building was erected on the same site in 1884.*

Also found at Christ Church Frederica are the graves of some of the plantation and slave owners. One of these is John Couper along with his wife, Rebecca, and daughter Isabella. John Couper of Scotland arrived in the United States in 1775 and moved in 1796 to St. Simons Island, where he established a plantation called Cannon's Point that was very successful in sea-island cotton.[76] Cannon's Point is now owned by the St. Simons Land Trust and is a 608-acre nature preserve that visitors are welcome to tour on select days of the week.[77]

St. Ignatius, the outreach of Christ Church Frederica, was built in 1886 for the freed slaves of St. Simons Island, in memory of Reverend Dodge's wife, who had died in India.[78] Reverend Dodge became its first rector and served in that capacity until 1898, when he passed away.[79] Although St. Ignatius was damaged in a hurricane, it was rebuilt in 1898.[80] The church is a beautiful historic building composed of natural interior wood patina, stained-glass windows, carved wood and religious décor.

St. Ignatius was headed by Deaconess Anna Ellison Butler Alexander, the first black deaconess of the Episcopal Church. She was from the Butler Plantation on St. Simons Island, where she had been born in 1865, the year the Civil War ended. Her mother and father lived in the area, but she went with the Episcopal congregation and taught school at Ignatius. She taught both black and white children at St. Ignatius Church and was said to visit homes of parents within walking distance to convince them that their children needed education. When they were going to finish school, she also got these children scholarships to attend historically black colleges and universities.[81]

She was the head of the church for a long time before she moved to the Sterling neighborhood in Brunswick, where she was the head of the Good Shepherd Church in the early 1900s. She used to walk a lot, and she used to go north for meetings for the Episcopal Church. One of the stained-glass windows in the church depicts Deaconess Alexander. It was installed there in 2001 and created by the artist Mary Beth Keys. Deaconess Alexander passed away in 1947, was named a saint of Georgia by the Diocese of Georgia in 1998[82] and was given sainthood by the Episcopal Church in 2018.[83]

Because the only men who knew construction at the time it was built were sailors and shipbuilders, the church is put together without any nails. African Americans were only allowed to go to Christ Church Frederica (the mother church) for the 3:00 p.m. service, so they attended this smaller church instead more regularly.

St. Ignatius Church. *Patrick Holladay.*

Emmanuel Baptist Church

This church was started in 1890 and is the third-oldest African American church on St. Simons Island. Originally, First African Baptist and Emmanuel had the same pastor. Each month, the pastor would preach two Sundays at one church and two Sundays at the other. When the pastor was at First African Baptist, Emmanuel didn't have services. The original building was destroyed by flooding in 1898 but was rebuilt by the congregation.[84]

Emmanuel came out of First African Baptist because the women said it was a long, hard ride all the way to First African Baptist twice a month. And when the men came up, they preferred to wander off to go hunting and fishing because they didn't want to go to church. Typical, right?

When kids left service at Emmanuel, they would go down to a house on George Lotson Street, where the Holiness Church would meet at times. This was because the children did not want to go home. They would see the Holiness Church members beating drums and jumping and shouting in their worship. The other big draw for the children was that the Holiness Church would give the kids a piece of candy. The kids had a good time and didn't get into any trouble. After church, the Holiness members would make sure the kids would go home. There was

Emmanuel Baptist Church. *Patrick Holladay.*

Emmanuel Baptist Church, circa 1959. *Amy Roberts.*

a telephone system without telephones. Everybody knew everybody, and everybody knew everything. It was a "village." Speaking of getting into trouble, a child could go home and find a parent or grandparent waiting on the porch for them. They would often wonder how they knew they had gotten into trouble because there were no phones. But word spread fast because of that village system.

St. Paul Baptist Church

St. Paul Missionary Baptist Church is located at 2700 Demere Road. St. Paul is the second-oldest African American church on St. Simons and was established in 1878. Like the congregation at First African Baptist Church in St. Simons, St. Paul came out of First African Baptist Church in Brunswick that was on Amherst Street, which is the oldest African American church in Glynn County. They, like their fellow church mates from the more northern

St. Paul Baptist Church. *Patrick Holladay*.

part of the island, found the rowboat trips back and forth to the mainland to be very difficult. Their initial services were held under an oak tree on St. Simons until a regular church building was constructed.[85] They also have an annual anniversary dinner that other churches attend.

Holiness Church

The Holiness Church is on South Harrington Road (the same road the Historic Harrington School is on) but is abandoned now. The congregation of that church also met in a house on George Lotson Street in the South End; they liked to move around and go to different locations.

HAZEL'S CAFÉ

Hazel's Café is located at 1166 Demere Road. It is a wooden building with a fading painted name across its front that reads, surprisingly enough, "Hazel's Café." Hazel Floyd worked at the shipyard in Brunswick helping to build Liberty ships during World War II. The Liberty ships are one of the port city's claims to fame, and ninety-nine of these cargo ships were constructed in Brunswick between 1943 and 1945.[86] There is a small replica statue located at Mary Ross Waterfront Park in historic Brunswick for the curious to see what they looked like. There is also a historic marker near the replica, on the intersection of Bay and Gloucester Streets:

> *During World War II, the J.A. Jones Construction Company operated a plant approx. 1 mile south of this point on Brunswick's waterfront. Between 1942 and 1944, a skilled labor force of over 16,000 men and women worked in service to the Allied war effort, producing 99 steel vessels for the U.S. Merchant Marines. These vessels served as both cargo and troop carriers, and their reputation for keeping vital supply lines open earned them the name of "Liberty Ships." Each month, dedicated shipyard workers produced four of these 447-foot, 3500-ton steel vessels. During December, 1944, with the "Battle of the Bulge" raging in Europe, the Navy requested six ships. In response, these determined patriots built an astounding seven "Liberty Ships." The J.A. Jones Construction Company and the people they employed in Brunswick's shipyards came to symbolize the patriotic duty and tireless efforts of America's wartime home front.*

When the shipyard closed down, Hazel Floyd decided to go into business on her own. She started the store and café in the 1940s with her husband, Thomas Floyd, who was a direct descendant of slaves brought to the Golden Isles on the *Wanderer* slave ship. The café eventually closed in 1978 after

Hazel's Café. *Patrick Holladay.*

Hazel and Thomas
Floyd. *Amy Roberts.*

nearly thirty years in business. Next door to the café is a small green house that Hazel and Thomas lived in. Many of Hazel's dishes were favorites of islanders, including sandwiches, fried fish and an amazing deviled crab (a boiled and stuffed crab recipe that is called "devil" because of the inclusion of hot pepper).

The café was mainly for takeout food, but sometimes people would eat outside the restaurant. There were also occasional barbecues and Lowcountry boils (a one-pot mélange of boil seasoning, corn, potatoes, sausage and shrimp) beside the café.

A local reporter, Larry Hobbs, once quoted Amy Roberts about Hazel's. She said, "This was a jamming little place.…There was a rooming house across the street, then there was the Jackson Apartments on other side of where that brick home is now. There were juke joints and Wilma's Theater, the Pavilion and the Atlantic Inn, which was down by the [St. Simons Elementary] school. It was all African American, of course."[87] The café and home next door are now in private ownership, but visitors are allowed to pull off and look at the café. Much of the interior of the café still reflects its history, with many of the decorations and artifacts still within the store.

PART III
JEKYLL ISLAND

Jekyll Island was named by General James Oglethorpe for his friend Sir Joseph Jekyll in 1734. Joseph Jekyll, a member of the British Parliament, a judge on England's Supreme Court of Judicature and knight of the crown, had been a generous financial donor to Oglethorpe's Georgia colony.[88] One of the first major landholders was Major William Horton, who was one of Oglethorpe's officers. Horton established a large plantation on Jekyll Island; the ruins of Horton's tabby house and some outbuildings are still standing on the island and open to tour. Following the Revolutionary War, the island was acquired by the Dubignon family in 1794 under the direction of Christophe Pulain Dubignon, a French nobleman who fled France to Georgia during the French Revolution.[89] Two of his descendants were complicit in the horrific *Wanderer* slave ship incident described later in this chapter.

The Dubignon family owned Jekyll Island for about a century and then sold the island to a group of wealthy businessmen that included William K. Vanderbilt, Cornelius Rockefeller II, J.P. Morgan, Marshall Field and Joseph Pulitzer. These men established the Jekyll Island Club. (There is more on the Jekyll Island Club later in this chapter.) The club ended its activities following the 1941 attack on Pearl Harbor, and the island was subsequently purchased by the State of Georgia. Most of the island was made into a state park in 1947. The history of the purchase of the island is inscribed on a plaque near the intersection of Riverview Drive and Stable Road and reads:

Melvin E. Thompson, Acting Governor, 1947–1949, was born in Millen, Jenkins County, Georgia, in 1903. After a career as educator and public servant, Thompson was elected Lieutenant Governor for the term beginning January, 1947. Following the death of Governor-Elect Eugene Talmadge, shortly before his inauguration, Thompson became Acting Governor until the next scheduled general election. During his term as Acting Governor, one of his contributions to the state was the acquiring of Jekyll Island for $675,000. The state acquired Jekyll Island by a court condemnation decree, a bargain which has been compared to the original purchase of Manhattan Island. Jekyll Island has proved to be one of Georgia's Greatest assets as a year round resort area

Jekyll Island State Park is run by the Jekyll Island Authority, a self-financed state organization that operates under the mission, "As stewards of Jekyll Island's past, present and future, we're dedicated to maintaining the delicate balance between nature and humankind."[90] The Jekyll Island Authority has been proactive and positive in promoting African American history on the island with the Wanderer Memory Trail, the Jekyll Mosaic Museum and interpretive signage at the 4-H Center that discusses places like the Dolphin Club and Hotel and the St. Andrews Auditorium. Each of these is discussed more in this chapter.

The Wanderer Memory Trail

The Wanderer Memory Trail is on the south end of Jekyll Island and can be accessed at St. Andrews Beach. There is a parking area, and then the memory trail winds along the dunes beside the beach and ends at a large watch tower. The Wanderer Memory Trail opened in November 2018 under the leadership of the Jekyll Island Authority. There was a *Wanderer* slave ship metal sculpture, built in 2008 as a memorial at St. Andrews Beach, but over time, it showed wear from all the salt air and exposure, so it had to be taken down.

The trail follows Umwalla, a fictional African boy who is presented as a captive who was brought to America from West Africa on the *Wanderer* slave ship. As the visitor walks down the memory trail, there is an interpretive story of Umwalla that follows his story from being captured in his African village to being sold at auction.[91] This story of his sale is a terrible travesty

The *Wanderer*. *Golden Isles CVB*.

not just because of the human, moral and ethical wrongs but also because the importation of African people was outlawed by Congress in 1808.

Yet laws like these were ignored by the greedy mercenaries who dealt in illegal activities like the slave trade and ships like the *Wanderer*. The *Wanderer* was a luxury schooner first built in 1857 by a wealthy member of the New York Yacht Club named Colonel John Johnson. When it was finished, it was said to be the fastest and best built yacht in existence. John Johnson ultimately sold the ship to Captain William C. Corrie of Charleston, who worked with a Charles Lamar of Charleston. Lamar had inherited a sum of money from his father but was a terrible businessman prone to racking up large debts, so he turned to the illegal slave trade. Lamar hired William Corrie to retrofit the *Wanderer* from a yacht into a slave ship with holds for captive people and extra water—two tanks that held fifteen thousand tons of water. On September 16, 1858, the *Wanderer* set sail from West Africa.

The *Wanderer* was the last slave ship to arrive in Georgia in 1858, with nearly five hundred enslaved West Africans who were brought up the Congo River and put on board. Most of these people were purchased from brokers who worked with tribal leaders who had captured these prisoners in war and sold them for cash, gunpowder and alcohol. The slave ship owners were terrifically cruel and "tight packed" the slaves into the hulls of the ship. A tight pack meant that as many people as possible were squeezed into the ship; by many calculations, the amount of room that an individual had on the *Wanderer* was about eighteen inches.[92] The slavers were banking on the speed of the *Wanderer* to bring as many enslaved West Africans to America alive as possible. Sadly, somewhere around eighty people lost their lives in passage. A survivor of the harrowing trip, one Charles Carr, said that as many as fifteen people who had died were thrown overboard on some days.[93]

Corrie and Lamar collaborated with John and Henry Dubignon, who owned Jekyll Island, to use the island as a place to bring the slaves they had captured.[94] The *Wanderer* arrived on Jekyll Island on November 28, 1858, after being at sea for forty-two days. When the slave ship arrived at Jekyll Island, the slaves were secretly sold to plantation owners and carried throughout the South. Many stayed in the Golden Isles and a few on Jekyll Island, but some were taken inland to places in Georgia and South Carolina. Some of the slavers who were crew on the ship, Nicholas Brown, Juan Rajestam and Michael Arguirir, aroused some suspicions when they were frequenting an establishment in Savannah, Georgia, and were subsequently arrested.

In December 1858, Captain William Corrie fled after Brunswick authorities began to find mounting evidence that the *Wanderer* had indeed been illegally used as a slave vessel. On February 25, 1859, the ship was decreed a slave ship by U.S. district judge J.C. Nicholl. The ship was seized and put up for auction in March 1859. Charles Lamar himself, sadly and ironically, was able to buy back the *Wanderer* at that very auction. He turned the sale around quickly and sold the ship to Captain David Martin, who sailed the ship away without paying.

The *Wanderer* memorial site. *Patrick Holladay.*

William Corrie, Charles Lamar, Henry Dubignon, John Dubignon and co-conspirators Nelson Towbridge (who outfitted the *Wanderer*) and John Tucker (one of the investors in the ship) were all charged with crimes related to illegal slavery, but none was ever convicted and all were acquitted on May 28, 1860.[95] This is likely attributable to bribery, corruption and proslavery attitudes in the region.

The *Wanderer*, after being hijacked by Captain Martin, was headed to Africa to be used in slavery again, but his crew mutinied and brought the ship back to Boston, where authorities eventually took ownership. The *Wanderer* was later used in the Civil War in 1861 by Union troops for carrying supplies and patrolling; following the Civil War, it was sold back into private ownership and was used to carry fruit until it sank off the coast of Cuba in 1871.[96]

THE JEKYLL ISLAND MOSAIC MUSEUM

The Jekyll Island Mosaic Museum is located near the Jekyll Island Club Hotel at 101 Old Plantation Road. The museum is located in what was once the stables for the club members. The museum has undergone a $3.1 million renovation to the 8,300-square-foot building. It holds more than twenty thousand artifacts and is operated by the Jekyll Island Authority.[97] Among the museum's artifacts is the only surviving piece from the *Wanderer* slave ship, a kettle that was used to feed the enslaved West Africans. The museum has been used as the starting point for tours around Jekyll Island during Black History Month.[98]

JEKYLL ISLAND CLUB HISTORIC DISTRICT AND THE RED ROW

As was noted in the beginning of this chapter, the history of the island from colonial to modern times went from General James Oglethorpe's soldier William Horton, to the slave trade–complicit Dubignon family, to the millionaire Jekyll Island Club, to its current position as a Georgia state park. Throughout these eras, there has been a growth of Gullah Geechee culture from those West Africans who were captured and brought to the region to work on rice and cotton plantations. This culminated in the illegal transatlantic passage of the *Wanderer* slave ship.

The descendants of West Africa were the first slaves on Jekyll Island, and following emancipation, they worked in many service jobs like groundskeepers, maids, nannies, cooks, drivers and servers, among others. The growth in service jobs started around 1886, when the Jekyll Island Club was established on the island by tycoons like J.P. Morgan, Joseph Pulitzer, Marshall Field and William K. Vanderbilt. Many of the jobs

The Jekyll Island Club Hotel. *Patrick Holladay.*

were taken by the people in the Gullah Geechee community, and others were filled by European immigrants and locals. Wages were competitive if sometimes lower than the national average. A housemaid of African descent, for example, earned about twenty dollars a month and a waitress about twenty-five dollars a month.[99] The club had somewhere around 120 seasonal and full-time employees, but activities and other parts of day-to-day life were segregated.

The Jekyll Island Club members only used the island for short periods throughout the year. During the rest of the year, the year-round employees stayed on the island and made use of the amenities like the golf course and bike paths. Earl Hill, a Gullah Geechee employee and golf caddy in the 1920s, once remarked, "It was only three months out of the year that the members were there, the rest of the year, why only the employees had the use of the island. That's where I got my jump in golf, because the millionaires would use the golf course three months out of the year, the other nine months I would use it."[100]

The black servants of the Jekyll Island Club were allowed to live near the Jekyll Island Club and its surrounding cottages but in segregated housing.

This housing for the black Jekyll Island Club employees and their families consisted of ten homes that had vibrant red roofs, made from a type of roofing felt, and so were dubbed "Red Row." One of the reasons that the Jekyll Island Club built the homes was for employee retention, as many of the employees were leaving the island for better-paying jobs.[101] The club owners had consulted with Sim Denegal, a respected black employee who was the road repair and forest foreman and oversaw a crew of fifteen to eighteen men (and, incidentally, earned $100 a month in 1925). Denegal worked with them in 1916 to build the Red Row.[102] He also ran a commissary in the Red Row area that sold a variety of products to the club employees.

Within the Red Row were also a schoolhouse and a small church, and in 1930, one of the houses was converted into a dance hall known as the Piccolo House; it got its name from a type of jukebox or music box called a piccolo that had been brought home to the Red Row by professional golfer Earl Hill.[103] The church in the Red Row was called Union Church and had been moved into the community by the Jekyll Island Club when it built Faith Chapel in 1904 and club members began to use Faith instead of Union. Union Church itself was constructed in 1898, but the club members thought it was too small, so they built Faith Chapel.[104]

Red Row employees, circa 1930s. *Matthew Raiford.*

When the State of Georgia took over Jekyll Island to make it into a state park in 1947, residents of Red Row began to move away because there was no more Jekyll Island Club as it had been. The last of the Red Row houses disappeared by the late 1970s. Nowadays, the general vicinity of the homes would be near the old amphitheater, near the Jekyll Island Authority offices in the green buildings and somewhat adjacent to a Jekyll Island community garden.

DOLPHIN MOTOR HOTEL AND PAVILION

The Dolphin Motor Hotel and Pavilion no longer exist on Jekyll Island, but some terrific interpretive story signs can be found on the grounds of the Georgia 4-H Camp Jekyll at 550 South Beachview Drive. The 4-H camp, which does environmental education and youth camps, is located on the former grounds of the Dolphin Motor Hotel and Pavilion. The grounds are open, and a walk around the buildings on the sidewalks that interconnect them will lead to five unique and informative signs.

One interesting component of the Dolphin Hotel was the Dolphin Club, which had a restaurant and lounge for dining, entertainment and dancing. The Dolphin Club operated from 1959 to 1966 and was a big draw for musicians on the "Chitlin Circuit" like B.B. King and Clarence Carter. "Chitlin" is the name for big intestines and is a part of soul food and Gullah Geechee cuisine. Chitlin is also somewhat synonymous with the South and so was used as the label for the circuit of venues that African American musicians and artists toured during the segregated Jim Crow era.[105] One of the interpretive signs at Camp Jekyll reads:

> *The Dolphin Club Lounge is largely remembered for the popular music it drew to Jekyll Island, as part of the Chitlin Circuit. The Chitlin Circuit was a string of black owned nightclubs that flourished primarily in the South, during the time of segregation. These clubs provided safe places for traveling black entertainers to perform for black audiences.*

The accomplished Jekyll Island historian Tyler Bagwell laid out a thorough timeline of how people of color were able to access the island beaches and construct their own facilities.[106] According to Bagwell's chronology, everything started in 1950, when black community leaders asked

The Dolphin Club Lounge sign. *Patrick Holladay.*

for their own area for beach recreation, which the Jekyll Island State Park Authority agreed to. A beach on the south end of the island, now St. Andrews Beach, was designated, and in 1955, a beach pavilion called the Negro Beach House was built. Today it is referred to as the Jekyll Island Beach Pavilion. The Negro Beach House had changing rooms, a concessionary and a picnic site. Near the Negro Beach House, land was cleared by the Jekyll Authority for multipurpose use like shopping, golf and house lots. This also included the space where the Dolphin Motor Hotel would be built.

In order to build the hotel, a group of black business owners formed the St. Andrews Beach Corporation in 1956. They began fundraising and then construction in 1958. The Dolphin Club and Motor Hotel opened in 1959. It was a short-lived venture due to financial disagreements among the corporation members, and they dissolved the organization in 1959, the same year that the hotel was opened. The St. Andrews Beach Corporation dissolved in late 1959, and the Jekyll Island State Park Authority purchased the motel. That was not the end, however, of the journey for the Dolphin Motor Hotel.

The entire property was leased to Dave Jackson, a prosperous African American businessman from Adel, Georgia. Jackson had done very well for himself as a cattle rancher, the founder of the Farmers Merchant Bank in Adel, a trustee board member of the Citizens Bank of Atlanta and a grain supplier to corporations like the Purina Company.[107] He shaped the

Motor Hotel into a family business that was run by his sisters and nephews. Yet in 1966, when racial integration came to Jekyll Island, business slowed down considerably, and the Jackson family was forced to close down. In 1968, the Jekyll Island Authority reimagined the facilities into a place for youth camps, and in 1983, Georgia 4-H started using the location. A $17 million renovation in 2014 made the camp a state-of-the-art center with new cabins, a dining hall, an auditorium, classrooms and learning laboratories.[108]

DR. JAMES CLINTON WILKES AND ST. ANDREWS

Dr. James Clinton Wilkes was an African American dentist who lived in the Golden Isles in the 1950s and 1960s, although he was originally from Pennsylvania. Dr. Wilkes was a graduate of Howard University School of Dentistry and a member of the Glynn County, Chatham County, Georgia and American Dental Associations or Societies.[109] As both a local civil rights activist in the 1960s and a member of the Georgia Dental Society—a historically black organization—Dr. Wilkes was able to force the Jekyll Island Authority to build the St. Andrews Auditorium by inviting the Georgia Dental Society to have its annual conference on the island.[110]

This was during the segregation practice of "separate but equal," and the Jekyll Island Authority had no convention center for African Americans. Another of the interpretive signs on Camp Jekyll states:

> Built in just a month, the one-room tin auditorium did not have the modern conveniences available to the island's white guests. The auditorium lacked such luxuries as air-conditioning, a ballroom and a heated swimming pool. Although the St. Andrews Auditorium was considered unequal to the island's white-only facilities, the black community put it to good use. The 600-seat space provided opportunities for meetings, family reunions, dances, and concerts. For a short time, Jekyll Island's segregated South End was known for its fabulous entertainment. Following the integration of Jekyll Island in 1964, however, the auditorium grew less popular, as recreational facilities around the island became available to everyone. Musical legend Otis Redding, known as the "King of Soul," staged the last big concert at the St. Andrews Auditorium in 1964, marking the end of an era.

This construction of a hastily built conference center was not the first slight against African Americans on Jekyll Island that had unexpected outcomes. Another instance is also highlighted on an interpretive panel at Camp Jekyll:

On October 23, 1958, a coal mining disaster in Springhill, Nova Scotia trapped 174 men underground. The coverage of this disaster was the first international event to be broadcast live on television. In the hope of harnessing the media spotlight and promoting tourism to Georgia, state administrators invited the last 19 mine survivors and their families to Jekyll Island to recuperate and enjoy some southern hospitality. The gesture backfired, however, when Governor Marvin Griffin, a staunch segregationist, realized one of the miners was black. The black miner, Maurice Ruddick, was the last man rescued from the collapsed coal mine. Called "The Singing Miner," Ruddick kept spirits up by singing, joking, and praying with the men during the nine days they were trapped underground together. Governor Griffin said Ruddick must be segregated from the others during their stay in Georgia. The other miners wanted to refuse the trip, but Ruddick agreed to avoid ruining their vacation. The highly publicized trip highlighted differences in the island's segregated facilities. The contrast between Ruddick's experience and that of the other miners was clear as the media spotlight remained focused on the "Miracle Miners" of Springhill. Ruddick's fellow survivors and their families enjoyed the north end of the island, including a new hotel, swimming pool, and fine dining. Meanwhile several trailers were set up on the South End of the island for Ruddick, his wife, and their youngest children. In response, the local black community rallied to offer their heartfelt hospitality to Maurice Ruddick and his family and make them feel welcome. This generosity of spirit salvaged a difficult situation. When asked how it felt to be segregated, Ruddick diplomatically answered, "I seem to be enjoying myself just as much as the others." Sandra Martin Mungin was just a teenager at the time, but she vividly remembers how the local African American Community came together to welcome Maurice Ruddick and his family. Her father, Genoa Martin, helped organize activities in Ruddick's honor, including a fishing trip, dinner party, and a community gathering. Mungin contributed to festivities by babysitting the Ruddick children and dancing in the talent show. Mungin said that the community wanted to help the Ruddick family enjoy their visit— in spite of segregation. The Ruddick family appreciated the overwhelming community support. When Mungin called Mrs. Ruddick later in life to reflect on their time on Jekyll Island, she said "I'll never forget it as long as I live! We had the most wonderful time!"

The home of Dr. Wilkes, although private property these days, can be seen on the south end of Jekyll Island near St. Andrews Beach on South Beachview Drive. He built the home in 1964 and enjoyed it for a number of years until his death in 1969. The very first home built in this neighborhood was erected in 1963 by Genoa Martin and his wife, Mamie.[111] Genoa was the director of Selden Park, which is described in detail in part IV.

The location of the homes is of no great surprise. It was the construction of the Dolphin Hotel and the Dolphin Club, along with the St. Andrews Auditorium, that turned the area near St. Andrews Beach into a thriving African American neighborhood. The neighborhood was of particular importance because it gave African Americans a place to vacation, find lodging and enjoy entertainment during the Jim Crow era of segregation in the South. The historic marker at Camp Jekyll related to this reads, in part:

> *In 1950, a group of African Americans from Brunswick requested that a portion of the island be made available for black people to enjoy. As a result, an area on the South End of Jekyll Island was reserved for African*

Dr. J. Clinton Wilkes's home. *Georgia Department of Economic Development.*

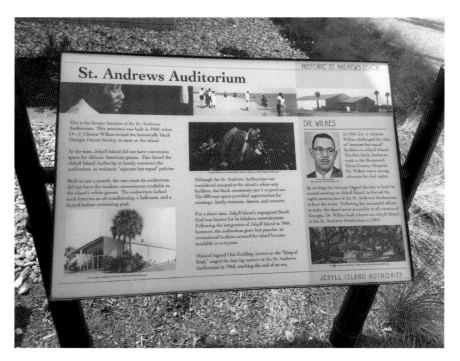

Dr. J. Clinton Wilkes sign. *Patrick Holladay*.

American use. It was named St. Andrews Beach. St. Andrews Beach was
the only public beach open to African Americans in Georgia and one of only
a few such beaches on the East Coast.

Also found on that historic marker is the name Jim Bacote. Jim Bacote was instrumental in the racial integration of Jekyll Island in his youth. In 1963, Jim, Reverend Julius C. Hope and W.W. Law (both presidents of branches of the NAACP) were denied access to a golf course, swimming pool and lodging. This quickly led to a lawsuit that ruled that any state-operated facilities on Jekyll Island must be integrated.[112] Bacote is a descendant of Dembo, an African who was enslaved somewhere in Gambia in 1783. Jim Bacote grew up in Brunswick near his future wife, Pat Bacote, who was a descendant of Bilali Muhammed of Guinea (Bilali was an educated man and quickly rose to the head of his plantation).[113]

The Bacotes were also the founders of the Geechee Kunda Cultural Arts Center and Museum on their family property in Riceboro, Georgia. Geechee Kunda has exhibits, classes, workshops, festivals and more, including an impressive collection of African and local artifacts. Geechee Kunda's founding was in part to "preserve and perpetuate the knowledge of important elements of African Culture that exists in the United States."[114] Jim Bacote passed away on May 6, 2018, and is buried in Greenwood Cemetery in Brunswick. There is an African proverb that says, "When an old man dies, a library burns to the ground,"[115] which is certainly the case with Jim Bacote.

Building on the Bacote story and the impact of desegregation on Jekyll Island, we look at another instrumental figure by the name of Earl Hill. Hill was a caddy for whites at the Jekyll Island Club in the 1920s.[116] After Jekyll Island was desegregated in 1964, Hill organized a golf tournament on the island along with a social club called the Frontier Club.[117] Hill was born in Glynn County, went to the Selden Normal and Industrial Institute and was an owner of the Blue Inn,[118] a popular club on the South End of St. Simons Island.[119]

The tournament was named the Southeastern Golf Tournament (nicknamed "The Classic") and became one of the Southeast's biggest tournaments.[120] Hill and the Frontier Club were able to secure sponsorships and amenities for the tournament, as well as manage the event.[121] Some of the notable professionals of the time who attended were Lee Elder, Jim Dent, Nate Starks and Jim Thorpe, as well as Jimmy Devoe, the owner of the first

Historic St. Andrews Beach sign. *Patrick Holladay.*

African American golf school.[122] Other prominent professional golfers at the tournament included Ted Rhodes, Zeke Hartsfield and Charlie Sifford.[123]

The very first tournament was funded in part by an Otis Redding concert that was held at the St. Andrews Auditorium.[124] That same year, however, the award ceremony for the tournament hosted "The Iceman" Jerry Butler, the original lead singer of The Impressions, who was an African American R&B singer. The ceremony and performance were held at the Jekyll Island Convention Center and not the St. Andrews Auditorium, which effectively desegregated the island's main event venue.[125] Other notable performers at the golf tournament's ceremonies over the years were acts like Wilson Pickett, Joe Simons and Percy Sledge.[126] Earl Hill hosted the tournament for nearly twenty years through the early 1980s until he passed away in 1985.[127]

PART IV

HISTORIC BRUNSWICK

The town of Brunswick began its European colonial establishment in the 1730s when Mark Carr, a captain in General James Oglethorpe's Marine Boat Company, started his plantation on the Turtle River in 1738. In 1771, Mark Carr's land was purchased by the Royal Province of Georgia, which planned it into a grid style in the same way that Oglethorpe had designed Savannah. Brunswick is still the second-biggest port city in Georgia, after Savannah, and was important for lumber, cotton, indigo and rice in the 1800s.[128] There are two historic markers for Mark Carr in Brunswick. One is in the median near the intersection of Union Street and First Avenue and reads:

> *Brunswick's first settler came to Georgia in 1738 with Oglethorpe's regiment. He was granted 500 acres at this place, on which he established his plantation. Several tabby buildings erected by him stood nearby and a military outpost was maintained here. In 1741 Indians from Florida raided his plantation, causing 750 pounds damage. The Indians killed or wounded some of the soldiers, while others were taken prisoners. 063-1 GEORGIA HISTORICAL COMMISSION 1953*

The other is a plaque embedded in brick from Carr's home and is on the grounds of the Brunswick Historic City Hall on Newcastle Street between Mansfield Street and Howe Street. The plaque reads:

Capt. Mark Carr, 1702–1767, Brunswick's First Settler, Came to Georgia in 1738 as an officer in the English forces located on St Simon's Island; established a plantation known as "Carr's Fields" and maintained a military outpost on the site of the City of Brunswick; assisted in repelling the Spanish invasion of 1742, and held many positions of honor and trust in which he gave loyal service to the Colony of Georgia. Brunswick Chapter DAR

Another smaller plaque on the side of the stone near the grounds reads, "The bricks used in this base came from the ruins of Capt Carr's home on Blythe Island."

The Gullah Geechee heritage of Brunswick has the same basic history as does that of St. Simons Island and Jekyll Island. Many of the African Americans who ended up on the mainland of Brunswick and Glynn County were originally enslaved West Africans who were forcefully brought to the Sea Islands. Some were brought to work on the mainland, while other Gullah Geechee people moved from the islands to the mainland over the years, especially after emancipation.

One of the greatest local recollections of black independence, self-sufficiency and community cohesion, in the early to mid-1900s, was a section in Brunswick around Gloucester Street and Albany Street known locally as "Black Wall Street." This was an area where black people where had established many businesses, including tax offices, barbershops and a funeral home. Many of the black community leaders like doctors, lawyers and teachers lived in the area. One important business was the Seagull Hotel, which was on the corner of Gloucester and Albany Streets. The Seagull Hotel was owned by Dr. R.N. Jackson, the only black doctor in the early 1900s. Dr. Jackson put a movie theater inside the Seagull Hotel, called the Jackson Theater, and was said to have allowed farmers and their families to pay for admission with produce.[129] The Jackson Theater closed in the 1930s, and the black-owned Roxy Theater became the movie destination for the community.

THE ROXY THEATER

The Roxy Theater sits in the Brunswick Old Town Historic District at the corner of Albany and F Streets at 1601 Albany Street and seats 250

Roxy Theater. *Georgia Department of Economic Development.*

people.[130] The theater was built in the 1940s and is among the older and historic African American theaters on record with the Georgia Historic Theatres Project.[131] The Roxy Theater was most popular during the 1950s and 1960s before eventually closing.[132] There was another theater in town called the Ritz Theater on Newcastle Street (which is still there and run by the Golden Isles Arts and Humanities Association), but people of African descent had to enter through a back entrance and could only watch movies from the balcony seating.[133]

The Roxy was also a place for performances. Sandra Mungin recalled, "Really brings back memories for [me performing with my father], Geona Martin, and many others during the fifties in the 'Hits and Bits' shows…. Great, wholesome times….Also attended many Saturday matinees for 15 cents. Mr. Crittenton was the manager."[134] While the theater is not currently used to show movies, it still has some limited use for community activities.[135]

THE COLORED MEMORIAL SCHOOL/RISLEY HIGH SCHOOL

The Colored Memorial School/Risley High School was established in 1869 by Captain Douglas Gilbert Risley, the district commander in the Freedmen's Bureau office in Brunswick. Risley served as a Union soldier during the Civil War.[136] The buildings are on Albany Street, between H and I Streets, with Martin Luther King Jr. Boulevard behind them; the entire complex is in the Historic Brunswick District. There are three buildings altogether that make up the Colored Memorial School/Risley campus, which was listed in the National Register of Historic Places in 2002. The first building was the Colored Memorial School, built in 1923. Next came Risley High School, now called Risley Elementary School, which was built in 1936. The last is the I Street Elementary School, which changed its name to the Jackson Building; it was an addition built in 1944. There is a historic marker outside the school that reads:

> *Brunswick's first public school for African Americans opened in 1870 as the Freedmen's School, later changed to Risley School to honor Captain Douglas Gilbert Risley, who raised funds for the school's construction. In 1923 the adjacent building, Colored Memorial High School, was built and named to honor African-American veterans in World War I. In 1936 Risley High School was built on the site of the 1870 Freedmen's School and remained in service until 1955 when a new Risley High School was constructed. Both the Colored Memorial School and Risley High School are landmarks of African-American education in Glynn County.*

The school is partially boarded up because the roof is leaking and the finances for repairs have not been found yet. The building is locked at all times, so visitation to parts of the school is very limited. However, one

Risley School. *Patrick Holladay.*

portion of the building is used by Coastal Pines Technical College for Adult Education classes and training. The center of the school houses the Risley Alumni Association and many artifacts from the history of the school. Items like photos, yearbooks, trophies and the like can be found here. Contact the Risley Alumni Association to schedule a time to see these artifacts.

Risley was named for Captain Douglas Gilbert Risley, who came to the area in the 1800s. He purchased the property and built the school. It was originally named the Freedmen's School but was renamed after Risley's death in honor of him. The Colored Memorial School was added in honor of World War I veterans in 1922. It was used as a high school, but as time passed, it became the school for the lower grades.

The part of the building where the alumni center is located was built in 1936 and held grades six through twelve. This portion of the building was the library. In 1955, grades eight through twelve moved to another high school in the 2900 block building, or the new Risley. There was a point when the school was used for two sessions a day. There were two groups of students; one group went to school from 8:00 a.m. to noon, and the other group went from 1:00 to 4:00 p.m. This was because the school had become overcrowded. However, this did not last long, and at some point, a regular daily session was reinstituted.

Indeed, after Perry Elementary School was built, some students from Risley (depending on where they lived) moved over to the Perry school in the 1950s. Students who attended Risley who were from outlying areas like St. Simons Island, Brookman and Sterling were bused in on public school buses. Grades one through seven were taught in various schools around the county, and then students in grades eight through twelve all came to Risley.

Since the buildings are in the National Register of Historic Places, the future or legacy for the school is to renovate the buildings that are closed off to the public. The Risley Alumni Association would like to make it into a fully operational museum that begins in the 1800s when the school started. It will house all the artifacts from over the years the schools were in operation. The association would also like to showcase what Risley graduates have accomplished. There have been, for example, six college presidents who graduated from the Risley School. Numerous doctors, lawyers and military veterans were also graduates. In addition, the association would also like to have an event space for alumni.

The history is also of importance, particularly regarding the involvement of the Freedmen's Bureau and the fact that Risley Colored Memorial was a Rosenwald school. The Risley Alumni Association, a 501(c)(3) nonprofit organization that was incorporated in 1992, is active and every year gives scholarships to students from local high schools as part of its organizational mission.[137] There are somewhere around five hundred members of the association. One challenge in the renovation is that the Glynn County Board of Education has to be involved and make decisions on what happens to the property because the board owns the property. As with most things, it boils down to the budget, and finding the funds for any work on the property has been problematic.

The Selden Normal and Industrial Institute

The Selden Normal and Industrial Institute is now a county park called Selden Park. It is located at the intersection of Norwich and Fourth Streets near Historic Downtown Brunswick at 100 Genoa Martin Drive. It is situated alongside the Turtle River. The Selden Normal School was the idea of Reverend Samuel G. Dent when he was a student at Morehouse

College in Atlanta. He then shared the idea with Reverend H.A. Bleach, who became the principal of Selden. Miss Carrie E. Bemus was the first teacher. This all started in 1892.[138]

The Selden Normal and Industrial Institute was established in October 1903. Miss Bemus found the site for the school to be built, which was about seventy acres. In 1909, Miss Bemus left the school due to age and failing health. Reverend Bleach then became the principal and expanded the teachers' training program and added music, business and athletics. Reverend Bleach passed away in 1918, and his successor was Reverend S.Q. Mitchell. Graduates of Selden went into teaching, theology, business, government and medicine. One graduate, Freeman Hankins, became a state senator in Pennsylvania. John H. Alston II became a senior analyst for Bell Laboratories.

In 1916, the Department of the Interior, Bureau of Education gave these details in a report called "Negro Education: A Study of the Private and Higher Schools for Colored People in the United States":

The Selden Normal School, which has recently moved to the suburbs, should be developed as a central training institution where pupils may board and supplement the training received in the rural schools. SELDEN NORMAL SCHOOL. Principal: H.A. Bleach. A school of elementary and secondary grade. It was founded in 1903 and is owned by the Presbyterian Board of Missions for Freedmen. The school has an independent board of trustees. It is supported in part by the Presbyterian Board and until recently received small appropriations from the American Missionary Association of the Congregational Church. Attendance. Total, 130; elementary 90, secondary 40. There were 30 pupils boarding at the school. Teachers. Total, 9; all colored; male 3, female 6. Organization. Elementary: Pupils are admitted as low as the fourth grade. The elementary classes are fairly well taught. Secondary: The three-year secondary course includes Latin, English, mathematics, agriculture, physiology, history, elementary science, psychology, and industrial work. Industrial: Instruction in sewing and cooking is provided for all the girls. The industrial work for boys consists of farm labor. Financial, 1914–15. The books and records are kept in accordance with the requirements of the Presbyterian Board of Missions for Freedmen. The more important items for the year were: Income, excluding noneducational receipts: $3,920; Expenditures, less noneducational receipts: $3,920; Value of plant: 15,544. Sources of income: Board of Missions, $3,013; tuition and fees, $486;

donations, $277; rallies and entertainments $107; other sources, $37. The noneducational receipts amounted to $3,353, of which $3,096 was from the boarding department and $257 from the farm. Items of expenditure: Supplies for boarding department, $3,773; salaries, $2,431; fuel and other supplies, $491; outside labor, $200; furniture, $154; books, stationery, and postage, $101; music department expenses, $95; repairs, $15; taxes, $6. Plant. Land: Estimated value, $5,000. The school land comprises 57 acres near the town. A part of the land is used for farm purposes. Buildings: Estimated value, $10,000. There are three buildings on the grounds. They are in good repair. Movable equipment: Estimated value, $544. The equipment consists chiefly of classroom and dormitory furniture. Recommendations. That the school make ample provision for teacher training and the theory and practice of gardening. Dates of visits: December, 1913; January, 1916.

The very first teacher at the Selden School was Miss Carrie E. Bemus, who was born in 1858. She had plenty of teaching experience, having taught at Morehouse College for eleven years. Miss Bemus had a friendship with the Selden family, in particular with E.P. Selden and his brother Dr. Charles Selden, a medical missionary to China. The Seldens were philanthropists and offered financial support for the founding of the school. The Selden Institute was born from a meeting in Brunswick at the First African Baptist Church, where Reverend Samuel G. Dent was elected chairman. A board of directors was formed with a Charles Shaw, who became a member as an influential businessman in the area. The school was named Selden Institute for Dr. Charles Selden. Some of the other teachers of record besides Miss Bemus were Maggie Rogers from Spellman College, Frankie Williams from Fisk University, Ella Porter-Bohannon from Western College and Frances Coleman from Howard University.

Miss Bemus purchased the sixty-five acres with her own savings and planned both buildings and land for cultivating food crops like sweet potatoes. The buildings and grounds construction were funded by Dr. Charles Selden, the school's namesake. Students paid modest enrollment, room, board and incidental fees. Students also gave one hour of service work a day. A student wrote in memoriam at the time of Miss Bemus's death and funeral, "We can look back along the years of Miss Bemus' life and see the hand of God leading her down every road that her feet have trod."[139]

The very beginning of the Selden Normal and Industrial Institute, starting in October 1903 before other construction had been completed, was in a brick building that was once used as a saloon. The courses of instruction included literacy, teacher's professional, sewing, music, millinery, business, dressmaking, domestic science, carpentry and agriculture. The institute was the equivalent of a junior college. The curriculum was technical in nature, with programs in areas like horticulture and homemaking. Girls learned basket weaving, knitting, sewing and the types of skills that were valuable to a domestic situation. Boys learned agriculture, planting, harvesting and the like.

The original headmaster was Reverend Mitchell, who started at the inception of the school along with Miss Bemus. One interesting fact is that Miss Bemus was also a tutor who would catch a ferry over to Sea Island, where she would teach lessons for her clientele. A couple of other pieces of history are that the school was torn down near the end of World War II, and the grounds were converted into a county park. Prior to the buildings' demolition, the school had ended its educational mission in 1933 when it merged with the Gillespie Normal School located in Cordele, Georgia.[140] In the park, however, the original gym remained, and there was a fabulous time from the late 1940s to the mid-1950s. Entertainers such as Sam Cook,

Headmaster's cottage at Selden. *Patrick Holladay.*

Percy Sledge, James Brown, Duke Ellington and Lena Horne came from all over on the Chitlin Circuit and played in the gym for the admiring crowds. Boxers like Cassius Clay and Tiger Flowers also visited. Much of this entertainment success was through the work of Genoa Martin, who was the director of Selden Park.

Along with the performances, every year all the churches from the area got together for an all-day picnic they called the "reunion." It was a major family event. The park was also used to a large extent as a daycare. Families used to bring their kids and drop them off at the park because they knew they would be safe while they were at work. A man named Homer Knight, who was a lifeguard, used to care for the children in the park. It is said that he taught over three thousand children how to swim. People knew if the kids were at the park they would stay out of trouble and stay away from the police. The park was more or less a refuge until the parents got off work.

There is some ongoing work to try to get the school in the National Register of Historic Places. The Selden Normal and Industrial Institute was considered one of the finest black educational facilities during the early twentieth century. The headmaster's cottage is the last piece of the Selden Normal and Industrial Institute. It is a one-story wood frame bungalow with Craftsman-style features, popular in Georgia between 1900 and 1930. There has been some partial rehabilitation by the Glynn County Recreation Department so that there could be a meeting space for the Coastal African American Historic Preservation Commission. This local commission's mission is to benefit and enrich the citizens and visitors of the city of Brunswick and Glynn County by raising awareness and promoting coastal African American history. The headmaster's cottage is currently vacant but does house historical artifacts from the school and the park. It is locked but can be viewed from the outside. It may be possible to look inside by calling the Glynn County Recreation Department and asking for entrance.

DIXVILLE HISTORIC DISTRICT

This is an area of great history on the south side of Brunswick that is in need of revitalization. This is a very interesting place and a good candidate for a driving tour to see a historic neighborhood full of vernacular architecture. There was a point in history when nearly 600,000 people lived here. This is a bit hard to wrap your mind around because the current population in

Brunswick is around 17,000 and county-wide only about 60,000 people. At one time, the south side of Brunswick was where the Liberty ships were built for World War II, and much of that huge population had moved to the area to work in the shipyards and factories.

Of the ten National Register–listed places of African American history in Glynn County, Dixville is the only historic district that is significant because of its ethnic heritage.[141] Dixville historic district is a good example of a planned residential community, established in 1875, for Brunswick's working-class, African American population.[142] Some of the interesting parts of the Dixville neighborhood are Dixville Park or Inez Williams Park and the ruins of the Glynn Ice Company. These ruins can be viewed from the street and are an interesting piece of the history of this place. The Glynn Ice Company was established in 1903 by R.C. Baumgartner and delivered ice to its customers with horse and buggy.[143] By 1907, the demand for ice had grown so much that the company was moved to a large facility on Newcastle Street in Brunswick. Inez Williams was a well-respected member of the Dixville community and was known as "the mayor of Dixville." She was responsible for a number of civic goods, including organizing the Red Cross at Friendship Baptist Church. Dixville Park was officially renamed Inez Williams Park in 2004.[144]

In 2017, Dixville was added to the Georgia Register of Historic Places; it is bounded by Walnut Avenue to the north, Palmetto Avenue to the east, Prince Street to the south and Martin Luther King Boulevard and Stonewall Street to the west.[145] This community was historically insular and self-supporting in nature. Everything one needed was there, like the barbershop, laundromat and grocery store. London, Gordon and Stonewall Streets had all the stores, the old icehouse, a theater (on the corner of Gloucester and MLK) and the playgrounds. This was near "Black Wall Street" (as described earlier), where a person could get all the economic work done with regard to real estate, insurance, taxes and the like.

A thorough description of the community is given in the nomination form for the Georgia Register of Historic Places regarding its significance from 1875 to 1967:

> *Shortly after the Civil War, displaced white planters from St. Simons Island first settled the Dixville neighborhood. However, by the 1880s, the planters had largely abandoned Dixville, and former slaves and white laborers began settling the low-cost, underutilized land. Residents were attracted to Dixville due to its proximity to available work at the nearby railroad,*

Historic ice plant in Dixville. *Patrick Holladay*

wharves, and sawmills. It became a unique example of a community where lower-income, black and white families co-existed throughout the late 19th and early 20th centuries. As pressures toward segregation increased, white residents left Dixville and by 1914, it had transitioned into a predominantly black community.

The Dixville Historic District is significant in the areas of black ethnic heritage as the only known intact, urban black community in Brunswick developed by both former slaves and white laborers. It contains a variety of resources that document residential patterns, and to a lesser extent, commercial and industrial development of Brunswick's black, working-class community from the late 19th century through the 1960s. Additionally, in the area of community planning and development, the district reflects land use patterns frequently associated with Georgia's cities whereby black and working-class settlement was relegated to under-utilized, low-cost land along the periphery of downtown. The district is also significant in the area of architecture for its collection of residential house types as identified in Georgia's Living Places: Historic Houses in Their Landscaped

Settings, a statewide context. Types found include shotguns, central hallway, gabled wing cottages/houses, Georgian cottages/houses, hall-parlor, and side-gabled cottages, as well as bungalows and ranch houses, representing the wide range of types popular between the late 19ᵗʰ to mid-20ᵗʰ century in Georgia.

The Dixville Historic District is an overwhelmingly residential neighborhood situated approximately one-half mile southeast of downtown Brunswick. The neighborhood was initially established c. 1875 but developed primarily during the New South period (c. 1880–1919), morphing into a cohesive African American community in the 1910s. The 41.3-acre district features a traditional grid-pattern layout with north-to-south dirt alleyways dividing many of the blocks. Most streets within the district are curbed and include concrete sidewalks. Lot sizes are relatively consistent, primarily ranging between 45 to 50 feet wide by 100 feet deep. The most prevalent house types represented are the ranch house and the bungalow. Other house types occurring in less frequent numbers include shotguns, central hallway, gabled wing cottages/houses, Georgian cottages/houses, hall-parlor, and side-gabled cottages. Residential stylistic influences within Dixville are limited, with Craftsman style being the most prominent. There are also a few examples of Plain style ranch houses and the Colonial Revival and Folk Victorian styles. The majority of buildings are wood frame, with brick veneer, weatherboard, vinyl, and asbestos being the most common exterior claddings. The district generally lacks formal landscaping and driveways are uncommon. Typical alterations include screening or enclosure of porches, window replacement, and application of vinyl siding. In addition to its many houses, the district also contains several commercial/industrial resources, religious facilities, and one public park. The most conspicuous of these non-residential resources is the Glynn Ice Company, a 1920 ice plant, with a condenser building and boiler house, located on George Street at the northeastern edge of the district. This industrial complex reflects the influences of Jacobethan Revival style with its shaped parapets, Flemish bond-patterned brick exteriors, and cast concrete trim. Dixville also includes a significant number of vacant lots; however, only seven of these were historically occupied by houses. Through its large number of intact resources and retention of the gridded street pattern, the district retains a high degree of historic integrity.[146]

The Communities of Brookman, Pennick and Arco

Brookman was settled during the late nineteenth century by the emancipated African slaves of area plantations. Like Dixville and the other Brunswick neighborhoods written about here, this area is best suited for a driving tour. Brookman is outside of Brunswick proper and is located on U.S. Highway 82 west of exit 29 off I-95. Many of the families who settled here after emancipation came from the Brunswick plantations like Laurel Grove, Bonaventure, Spring Hill, Reedy Branch and Magnolia.[147]

Many of the historic buildings like homes, churches, schools, stores and family cemeteries are still intact. One of these is the Union School, which is described in part V on the entry about Gilliard Farms, as the school sits on that property. Another is the Wright house and family cemetery, which were constructed around 1900 and are of quality to be listed in the National Register of Historic Places.[148]

Pennick is another more rural community that was founded by freedmen from area plantations such as Elizafield, which was one of the most prosperous of the rich Altamaha River plantations of the early nineteenth century.[149] Pennick was a predominantly African American settlement.

Lula and Arthur Wright house in Brookman, circa 1900s. *Robert Ciucevich.*

Good Shepherd Church and School in Pennick. *Robert Ciucevich.*

Craftsman bungalow in Arco. *Robert Ciucevich.*

One of the best historical sites in the community is the Good Shepherd Episcopal Church and Parochial School. As was described in part II, Deaconess Alexander was the one to come here and start this school after she left her work on St. Simons Island and St. Ignatius Church. She used to walk back and forth from Pennick to Darien, Georgia (another community in McIntosh County), to teach. She lived in a loft in the top of the church. When Glynn County decided to close the outlying schools, the Good Shepherd School was one such school. On the grounds of the church is a cross-shaped monument that marks the grave of Deaconess Alexander, who passed away in 1947 and was interred here. The church and school are considered examples of Italianate and Folk Victorian styles of the early twentieth century.[150]

Arco is one of the oldest neighborhoods in Brunswick and is a subdivision of working-class cottages and bungalows developed in the 1930s and 1940s east of Newcastle Street and U.S. Highway 341, opposite the nearby Atlantic Refining Company Plant. The name "Arco" comes directly from the name Atlantic Refining Company; that plant was demolished in 2008. Most of the Arco subdivision neighborhood is largely intact and appears eligible as a historic district.[151]

CEMETERIES OF BRUNSWICK

Greenwood Cemetery

Greenwood Cemetery is located off Highway 341 and is described as a historic African American cemetery in Brunswick.[152] The City of Brunswick's Cemetery Division does not have the records for exactly how big the cemetery is or the founding date. Further, burial records for the cemetery before 1965 are scarce.[153]

Greenwood Cemetery was established near the end of the 1800s as a place to memorialize black citizens of the time. The cemetery encompasses about thirty-five acres. Notable people buried here include Thomas Floyd, who, along with his wife, Hazel, owned and ran the popular St. Simons Island eatery Hazel's Café (described in detail in part II). Jim Bacote, the activist and community leader described in part III, is buried here as well. Also among the notables buried here is Reverend G.M. Spratling, who led

Greenwood Cemetery sign. *Patrick Holladay.*

Brunswick's black Baptist community in the late nineteenth century. Most of the oldest graves are to the front left of the cemetery. A few are even marked with wooden markers.

Oak Grove Cemetery

This cemetery rests at the northeast corner of the Dixville Historic District, off Martin Luther King Jr. Boulevard at 1500 Mansfield Street. Oak Grove Cemetery was established in 1838, and it might be the oldest existing public cemetery in Glynn County. The cemetery was originally planned to be ten acres in size but was scaled down to three acres in 1871. Of the 1,200 graves in the cemetery, 481 are unmarked and over 60 are unknown. In addition, around 200 Confederate and Union soldiers of the Civil War are buried here.[154]

Some prominent figures in African American history are buried here, such as Jackson K. Sheffield, who made his fortune as a sawmill owner and property owner, and Captain Douglas Risley, who established Risley Colored Memorial School. Risley served in the Union army during the Civil War.

HISTORIC BLACK CHURCHES OF BRUNSWICK

There are several African American churches in Brunswick that are part of the Brunswick Old Town National Register District. First African Baptist of Brunswick was founded in 1863 by worshipers who were meeting in a grove off Lee Street, between Gloucester and F Streets. The congregation built its church at 1416 Amherst Street in 1869. Its daughter church, St. Paul Baptist, stands at 1929 Albany Street. St. Paul African Methodist Episcopal (AME)

Shiloh Baptist Church. *Shiloh Baptist Church archives.*

Church, circa 1922 Gothic Revival edifice, stands at 1520 Wolfe Street in the Old Town District. St. Paul Baptist Church, the daughter church of First African Baptist of Brunswick, sits only three blocks outside the district's northern boundary at 1929 Albany Street. Grace United Methodist Church is located at 1711 Albany Street. It was founded on November 18, 1868. Shiloh Baptist Church is located at 1221 Egmont Street and was founded in 1873.

St. Athanasius Episcopal Church

This church is located at 1321 Albany Street at the intersection of Albany and Monck Streets in Historic Downtown Brunswick. The church is the second-oldest congregation in Brunswick and grew out of a mission started in 1885. By 1890, St. Athanasius was a self-sustaining parish led by Reverend J.J. Perry. St. Athanasius came out of the Episcopal Church and the local church called St. Marks. It first began under the direction of Louise Nightingale and Mary King Troupe of St. Marks Church as a Sunday school. The school became a parochial school that was instrumental in the education of African American children at the time. The school closed in 1928 following World War I. As with the Selden Normal School, there is a terrific description in the Department of the Interior, Bureau of Education's 1916 report called "Negro Education: A Study of the Private and Higher Schools for Colored People in the United States":

The St. Athanasius parochial school enrolls a large number of elementary and secondary pupils. It should center its efforts on secondary and industrial work for the city. ST. ATHANASIUS PAROCHIAL SCHOOL. Principal: W.A. Perry. A good elementary day school with a few secondary pupils. It supplements the inadequate public-school facilities. The school was founded in 1888 by the American Church Institute for Negroes of the Protestant Episcopal Church. It is owned by the Episcopal Diocese of Georgia and partially supported by the American Church Institute. Attendance. Total, 226. There were 15 pupils above the eighth grade. Teachers. Total, 14; all colored; male 1, female 13. Organization. The work covers 10 grades of regular academic work. In addition the girls have two hours a week in sewing and the boys above the sixth grade two hours in shoemaking. Financial, 1912 13. As far as could be determined the more important items were: Income $3,624; Expenditures, $3,624;

St. Athanasius Church. *Patrick Holladay.*

Value of plant $10,000; Sources of income: American Church Institute for Negroes, $1,800; Episcopal Board of Missions, $1,000; tuition and fees, $824. Items of expenditure: Salaries, $3,200; operating expenses, $424; Plant—Land: Estimated value, $8,500, The land consists of a large city lot. Building: Estimated value, $8,500. The only building is a neat two-story stucco building containing classrooms. There are no dormitory provisions. Movable equipment: Estimated value, $500. The equipment is limited to a small amount of classroom furniture. Recommendations. 1. That the theory and practice of gardening be made part of the regular course and the industrial course strengthened. 2. That the secondary course provide for teacher training. Date of visit: December, 1913. Facts verified, 1916.

The church was originally a tabby building, but a hurricane destroyed that building, and the one that stands there now was built in the 1930s. The school continued to develop itself and had dormitories, tennis courts and a well-maintained landscape. The school closed in 1928 when the state started funding money for the public school system.

The name of the church comes from St. Athanasius of Alexandria, Egypt, in the AD 300s. Inside the church are a number of stained-glass windows that serve as memorials. The people depicted in the stained-glass windows are of importance to the church, the community and the greater community. One of particular interest and uniqueness is the stained-glass window of Dr. Martin Luther King Jr. The church is part of the National Register of Historic Places, and tours of the inside can be made by contacting the church and setting up an appointment.

PART V

FURTHER EXPLORATIONS OF THE GOLDEN ISLES

HOFWYL-BROADFIELD PLANTATION STATE HISTORIC SITE

The Hofwyl-Broadfield Plantation (State Park) is located driving north away from downtown Brunswick on Highway 17. A driver approaching the park will see signs for the entrance on the right-hand side of Highway 17. The site offers a museum with a film in the visitors' center, a nature trail and a guided tour of the main antebellum plantation house and outbuildings. The grounds are easily walkable and lush with vegetation and hundreds of majestic live oaks. The live oak directly adjacent to the main house is believed to be in the neighborhood of eight to nine hundred years old. There is an admission charge and limited hours, so it is good to check on that ahead of a visit. The Hofwyl-Broadfield Plantation State Historic Site webpage does a really good job of describing the plantation:

> *This beautiful plantation represents the history and culture of Georgia's rice coast. In the early 1800s, William Brailsford of Charleston carved a rice plantation from marshes along the Altamaha River. The plantation and its inhabitants were part of the genteel low country society that developed during the antebellum period. While many factors made rice cultivation increasingly difficult in the years after the Civil War, the family continued to grow rice until 1913. The enterprising siblings of*

the fifth generation at Hofwyl-Broadfield resolved to start a dairy rather than sell their family home. The efforts of Gratz, Miriam and Ophelia Dent led to the preservation of their family legacy. Ophelia was the last heir to the rich traditions of her ancestors, and she left the plantation to the state of Georgia in 1973. A museum features silver from the family collection and a model of Hofwyl-Broadfield during its heyday. A brief film on the plantation's history is shown before visitors walk a short trail to the antebellum home. A guided tour allows visitors to see the home as Ophelia kept it with family heirlooms, 18th and 19th century furniture and Cantonese china. A stop on the Colonial Coast Birding Trail, this is an excellent spot to look for herons, egrets, ibis and painted buntings. A nature trail leads back to the Visitor Center along the edge of the marsh where rice once flourished.

The above description, however, does not explain the Gullah Geechee connection in much detail. In fact, as you read, that description states, "While many factors made rice cultivation increasingly difficult in the years after the Civil War…" The main reason was that there was no enslaved workforce to continue large-scale rice production. As was described in part I, the Gullah Geechee, as enslaved West Africans steeped in agricultural knowledge of rice production, would have been the backbone of this plantation. The plantation was built in 1807 as a large rice producer with over seven thousand acres of rice fields and more than 350 West African slaves.[155] The majority of the enslaved people of this plantation came from Sierra Leone and Senegal, according to local recollections.

The conditions that they had to work in must have been beyond hellish under the sweltering heat of the sun, waist deep in marsh water, feet dragging through muck and constantly plagued by mosquitoes and the fear of dangerous animals like water moccasins and alligators. Also, what may not be readily apparent when someone visits the plantation is that much of the marsh that became rice fields was riddled with cypress trees. These trees had to be logged by the slaves, and then they had to build a canal and dike system to control the tidal flooding and draining in the fields.[156]

There are also stories of compassion, such as the one of Dr. James Troup, who married into the family around 1813 by wedding Camila, the daughter of William Brailsford, who founded Hofwyl-Broadfield Plantation. Historical records indicate that Dr. Troup bought the neighboring New Hope Plantation for the express reason that he "neither wanted nor needed

Hofwyl-Broadfield Plantation House. *Golden Isles CVB.*

the New Hope slave but purchased them anyway for around $50,000 so they would not be sold at auction and families separated."[157] The purchase of New Hope Plantation brought the total family land between the two plantations to over seven thousand acres, but it was again parceled into smaller pieces (including Broadfield Plantation) following the death of Dr. James Troup, who willed it into three sections divided among his heirs.[158]

The rice fields of the nineteenth century were the economic center of coastal Georgia, but following the Civil War, they rapidly lost their footing as costs and the lack of slave labor took their toll. Compounding this were several crop failures in the 1860s, new types of mechanization, imported rice that was in competition with local rice and destruction caused by hurricanes that so frequently hit the Atlantic coast.[159] The owners of Hofwyl-Broadfield were persistent, however, and rice production continued until 1915, when they converted the rice plantation into a dairy farm that operated until 1942.[160]

Of interest to some is that Margaret Mitchell, author of *Gone with the Wind*, was a family friend and often visited the plantation.[161] Eventually, the plantation and its historic buildings became a State Historic Site in 1974 after Ophelia passed away and gave the plantation to Georgia. The almost two thousand acres of coastal land and marsh became a site in the National Register of Historic Places in 1976.

Beginning in the 1990s, archaeological excavations started around the buildings that are still there and also, even more importantly, around the buildings that were no longer there but could be found by their foundations and remnant parts.[162] Within these excavations, the archaeologists were able to find not only old artifacts but also the location of the slave settlement that was on the plantation. A report was produced about the archaeological study and stated, "Rice plantation slaves had more freedom than slaves on upland cotton plantations; part of this was due to the difference in work organization (the task system was used rather than the gang system) and also because the plantation master spent very little time on the plantation due to the serious threat of malaria."[163]

It has been noted that one of the extant slave dwellings has been converted into a restroom for visitors, which does not sit well with some. Along with this current issue, there are many historical accounts of the devastation felt by the enslaved West Africans on this plantation. For instance, there is an account of a hurricane in 1804 that killed seventy slaves[164] as they were swept up by the torrential water and howling winds to be drowned to death. There are also some sparse stories of the slaves from Hofwyl-Broadfield Plantation, pulled together by fragments of old documents. One is of Sam the carpenter:

> *I know Sam was caught in early September 1807 and sailed south two days later, presumably in irons, and I imagine William Crawford, the planter who bought him, sent boat hands to fetch his recalcitrant new slave. What became of Sam afterward is a mystery. Maybe William Crawford was a forgiving man who welcomed the young carpenter gently onto his plantation. Maybe he had Sam flogged. I'd like to believe the captive from Savannah found some pleasure in his new surroundings— maybe a wife, children, friends—and that these were not sold away from him nor he from them. Sam's story is one of countless narratives, small and large, that hint at the scope of the suffering endured by African Americans in the 17th, 18th, and 19th centuries. As Joe reminds us, there were over four million enslaved Americans at the end of the Civil War. That's a lot of sorrow.*[165]

Following emancipation, the freed slaves settled in small communities like New Hope and Petersville (named for the first freed slave who lived there), where they worked for wages at the same rice cultivation jobs they had as slaves. Petersville Cemetery, sometimes referred to as Broadfield Cemetery, is the resting place of the Africans who toiled at Hofwyl-Broadfield Plantation and their descendants. It is located off Highway 17 near the state historic site by following Petersville Road. While it is open to visit, it is in poor shape and highly overgrown with vegetation. Some markers can be seen, but many are buried and hidden under tangles of weeds, vines and tree roots. Also, the records of who is actually buried here are sparse, as local death records are not readily available.[166]

Another name for this cemetery may be Freedmen's Rest or Elizafield Burial Ground.[167] The names are sometimes interchanged in historical records. For example, an Elizabeth Chambliss is recorded as being buried in Broadfield Cemetery, but her headstone can be found in Petersville Cemetery. A Maggie Harris has her tombstone in Elizafield Burial Ground, but her death certificate says she is buried in Broadfield Cemetery.[168] It also seems that most of the people recorded to have been buried in Broadfield Cemetery can have their headstones found in what is locally known as Petersville Cemetery.[169] There are some speculations that these remains may have once been located on the grounds of what is now the Federal Law Enforcement Training Center (FLETC) and moved to this location (and that there might still be graves on FLETC property).

Needwood Baptist Church and School

This church is located off U.S. Highway 17 North as you travel away from Brunswick. Driving in this direction, the church and school will be on the left-hand side. You will see a white wooden church with three peaks in the roof, which are the main roof and two towers. The towers were constructed and added to the church around 1885, and in one of them is a church bell that was made probably around 1884.[170] The bell is said to have been cast in Baltimore and is considered a "treasure" of the church.[171] Next to the church, in the trees, is a smaller white building that was once the school. The building has fallen into terrible disrepair and is generally locked. Visitation of the site will be only on the grounds around the two buildings.

The church is a wonderful style of vernacular architecture. It is constructed of wood with tongue-and-groove boards for the walls and ceiling and has wooden floors. The frame is post and beam style, and the pews inside the church are original from the 1800s.[172] The church has a historical marker in the front that reads:

> *Needwood Baptist Church was organized in 1866 on nearby Broadfield Plantation as Broadfield Baptist Church of the Zion Baptist Association. This structure, built in the 1870s, was redesigned*

*in 1885 when the church moved its congregation here. Its formation
and history are representative of religious development in the context of
plantation rice culture. The nearby one-room Needwood School provided
elementary education for this community from 1907 until desegregation
in the 1960s. Both structures are examples of early African-American
vernacular architecture. Portions of this church were originally built by
freed slaves on the Broadfield Rice Plantation, where it was initially
the Broadfield Baptist Church, in the late 1870s. It is now considered
one of the better examples of African-American vernacular church
architecture remaining in Georgia. Erected by The Georgia Historical
society and the Pilot Club of Brunswick, Inc.*

The church and school were named for the Needwood community,
which was one of the communities that was established by emancipated
slaves from the Hofwyl-Broadfield Plantation. The name "need wood" was
quite literal. Apparently there was a shortage of "fat lighter," which is pine
heartwood that is dense with pine resin (resin is highly flammable) that was
often used to start warming or cooking fires. One of the cornerstone families
of the Needwood Baptist Church and school is the Polite family. The name
Polite extended all the way back to slave times when the patriarch of the
family adopted the name because he was well known for his politeness.[173]
One Morris Polite—who lived in the Petersville community with his wife,
Joan, and thirteen children—worked on the Hofwyl-Broadfield Plantation
along with his grandfather, father, children and grandchildren for five
generations.[174]

Morris had a son named London who was born into slavery but returned
to Hofwyl-Broadfield to work for the Dent family after emancipation; it is
assumed that London was one of the people who helped build Needwood
Baptist Church.[175] London had a son named William Polite who, in turn,
had a granddaughter named Alfreda Grant-White. When Alfreda speaks
of her grandfather William, she says things like, "When he spoke you would
think you were listening to the Book of Proverbs. He was full of words of
wisdom on how to live your life and how to conduct yourself."[176]

There is some speculation that the Needwood Baptist Church was
originally erected on the property of the Hofwyl-Broadfield Plantation
and then moved to its current location after the plantation landowners
gave land to the workers to have for themselves.[177] The school also played
an important role for the Gullah Geechee children who lived in the area;
it was nearly impossible for freed African Americans to find education

Needwood Church. *Patrick Holladay.*

following the Civil War in the rural part of the South. One of the teachers at the Needwood School in the 1940s and 1950s was Susie Anderson, who generally taught about fifteen children at a time; after the school closed in the 1960s, it served as a kitchen for the church, a community hall and more recently for storage.[178]

Alfreda Grant-White is also the spokesperson and advocate for the restoration of Needwood. The church and the school are deeply embedded into the memories, lives and community of the people here. As Alfreda's mother, Laura Polite-Short, said, "I was born out here and raised within the church. And I went to school here from first to seventh grade, before I transferred to Risley High in Brunswick."[179]

The church and school are in obvious disrepair, so much so that a nonprofit group called Rural Historic Churches of Georgia submitted the site to the National Trust for Historic Preservation's Most Endangered Places in America.[180] In November 2018, the Georgia Trust for Historic Preservation placed the Needwood Baptist Church and School on the state's 10 Places in Peril list. As the trust states, "Places in Peril is designed to raise awareness about Georgia's significant historic, archaeological and cultural resources, including buildings, structures, districts, archaeological sites and cultural landscapes that are threatened by demolition, neglect, lack of maintenance, inappropriate development or insensitive public policy."[181] Among the greatest structural threats are the collapsing roof and widespread water damage.

Since it is unlikely that a visitor will be able to enter either the church or the school, included here is a description of the church and school, including many of the details from the interior of the church that were included in the National Register of Historic Places Registration Form:

Needwood Baptist Church and School property contains a historic church building and a historic school. The church is a one-story, wood-frame, weather boarded building with a metal roof and two front square towers connected by an enclosed porch. The sanctuary occupies most of the church and is the oldest part, dating from the 1870s. The towers, added c. 1885, contain bathrooms on the lower level and, in one, a bell, dated 1884. In the 1918 rear addition is a small pastor's room, with its own side entrance and porch, and the pulpit area. The ceilings and walls are tongue-and-groove board. A plywood floor covers the original floor. There is vertical wainscoting. Thirty original pews remain as do other church furnishings: a pastor's chair, pulpit, table and spittoon. Changes to the church include the enclosure of the front porch in the 1930s. Electricity was added in 1937. Early church members recall the interior being blue, a color long painted over. The other building on the property is a one-room, frame, pre-1907 schoolhouse later used as a church fellowship hall. The school has a single entry door facing the highway and windows on one side. It has masonry tile siding and retains an original blackboard and desks. The church and school are located in a rural setting along a major road.

The interior consists of the anteroom (originally an open entryway), the rooms on the lower levels of the towers, now used as bathroom, and a large sanctuary at the rear of which is a room, open and connected to the sanctuary and used by the choir and for the pulpit, and an enclosed room used as the pastor's study. The interior is wood tongue-and-groove-board, both ceilings and walls. The floor is plywood which is said to cover the original wood planking. The wall boards are mounted horizontally, except for a wainscot of vertical boarding, approximately three feet high. All surfaces are painted. Lumber used in the construction is a mixture of hand-hewn timbers and milled material. The ceiling joists which span the width of the structure are hand-hewn timbers, while the rafters are mill-sawn lumber. Cut nails are used throughout the structure giving a date of construction earlier than 1890. The church contains many old furnishings and artifacts. There are approximately thirty dark pine wood pews which are said to be the originals. These show evidence of hand-sawn kerf marks and "whittle" marks on the side brackets. There is a charcoal sketch of three former pastors of the congregation on the back wall of the church. These are Rev. Tyson, Rev. Nelson and Rev. Neal. Rev. Andrew O. Neal [Neyle] was the first pastor, from the year of founding in 1866. Rev. Nelson served in the 1880s until his death in 1896–1897. He was succeeded by Rev. Scranton Roberts for one year and then by Rev. L.J. Tyson. The church also contains the old pastor's chair, pulpit, table and spittoon. Also the church retains an old baptism set and chalice.[182]

Gilliard Farms

Gilliard Farms is located west of historic Brunswick in the Brookman community (which is described in part IV). It can be reached by heading west on U.S. Highway 17 for about ten miles as you drive away from Brunswick. There is a left-hand turn off Highway 17 down Galilee Road. The farm is down that road, onto Gilliard Terrace and is recognized by a collection of homes, buildings and farm structures (like a hoop house and gardens). It is a good idea to call or e-mail ahead to make an appointment to visit. The farm is a working business and does not have established visiting hours.

Gilliard Farms is named for Jupiter Gilliard, who was born around 1812 in South Carolina and established the farm in 1874. Jupiter purchased 476 acres of land for nine dollars in tax costs; the current size of the farm is about 28 acres in production, as land has been parceled out over the years through marriages within the family to help newlyweds get started with their lives.[183] Gilliard Farms is a Centennial Family Farm (over one hundred years old), the only such in South Georgia and one of the oldest continually owned African American farms in the United States. Gilliard Farms was awarded the designation of Centennial Family Farm in Georgia in 2012 and was only the tenth African American–owned farm of the (at the time) 426 Centennial Family Farms recognized in the state.[184]

The farm is owned and operated by James Beard–nominated chef[185] Matthew Raiford; his partner, Jovan Sage; and Matthew's sister Althea Raiford. It was back in 2010, during a family reunion, that Matthew and Jovan had a conversation with their aunt Mary Lou and grandmother Ophelia about returning the property back to farm production;[186] it had not been farmed in decades. All three have deep roots in the land, and both Matthew and Jovan have been intimately involved in culinary food movements such as Slow Food, the international organization that promotes good, clean, fair food for all, and Seed Savers Exchange. Matthew is proud of the heritage of his farm; Jupiter Gilliard is Matthew and Althea's great-great-great-grandfather, and the chef will point out that when his children work on the land, they are the seventh generation of his family to do so. Growing up on the farm gave Chef Matthew a great appreciation for being outside and enjoying the practice of farming in nature.[187] Both Matthew and Althea are military veterans as well.

The military connection is an important one beyond an admiration for service. Matthew is quick to point out that professional opportunities as an African American male in the Deep South were quite difficult to come by.[188] It was the military that gave him his first entrance into the culinary world as a vocation and then onward to executive chef positions in prestigious places like the U.S. House of Representatives and Little St. Simons Island, which is a private island resort off the Georgia coast. From there, a multifaceted career covering nearly thirty years finally brought him home to Gilliard Farms. This, too, is very important, as black farmers in the United States make up only about 1.4 percent of all farmers in the country.[189] Althea Raiford is cut from similar cloth. She served in the navy for over twenty years, including deployments in Operation Desert Shield in Iraq and Kuwait.[190] She has noted that many military veterans have tremendous difficulties reentering the civilian world and that farming was a way for her to do that.[191] She tells her own story as an expression of her passion for Gilliard Farms:

> *I was the youngest among my cousins in GA. This meant I was often times left with my great-grandmother, Florine. Who would tell me stories of how our family had come to be part of the backbone of the community. The hard work and relentless spirit of those that came before me. She taught me how to take eggs from the hens in the backyard. Which by the way I was terrified that the chickens would peck me; I remember her putting her apron on me sending me in the coop and not allowing my fears*

to paralyze me. She taught a valuable life lesson, fight through your fear or go without reaching your goals. I spent many days and nights with her reading, writing and her listening to my childish dreams. She always encouraged me to dream big and never allow what others said deter me. I remember picking pears from our pear tree and making preserves. Picking up pecans for pie from our yard. My Nana, Ophelia, in the spring and summer would send me to our neighboring farms that she would get other vegetables from. I learned how to pick every kind of green, melons, peppers, and list goes on and on. While in the military whenever I would come home I would walk the property with my Nana and she too would share stories of life on the farm before I was born. Matthew and I are just picking up where our family left off, living off the land, building a stronger community, and taking care of those we love. My passion for Gilliard Farms comes from my love and appreciation for my family's legacy and my community.[192]*

In Michael Twitty's book *The Cooking Gene*, Matthew recounts the current cultivation of Carolina gold rice, Bradford watermelons, muscadines (which they make into shrubs, a type of vinegared drink), greens, peanuts, tomatoes, okra and Georgia red sugar cane, as well as livestock and wild game.[193] The muscadines have a particularly long heritage on the farm, as Jupiter Gilliard was the one who originally harvested them from the woods and planted them on the land.[194] Matthew (in Twitty's book) goes on to speak of the memories of catching a variety of seafood like shrimp, blue crab and oysters in the tidal creeks and how adding paprika to fish fry batter made the final product a rich gold color. Matthew's partner, Jovan, who is a master herbalist, will also point out all the herbs and wild plants that she uses to make teas, tinctures, prepared dishes and fermented products that cross the land.[195]

The land itself is unique not only in that it has stayed in the same family since that family found freedom through emancipation in the Civil War–torn South but also that it has stayed organic, sustainable and free of chemicals—they've never been used. These stewardship values come from Matthew's history with the land but also from education at the Culinary Institute of America and in the University of California–Santa Cruz's Center for Agroecology and Sustainable Food Systems. They also show up in Matthew's own label for himself as "CheFarmer."

Also unique to the farm was the establishment of a school called Union School. As a school for African American children in the area, it was a vital part of the fabric of the community and was constructed circa 1907.[196] The school was built on land owned by Matthew and Althea Raiford's grandmother Ophelia Johnson. It was a public school built by Glynn County and taught children from kindergarten through eighth grade. After the eighth grade, students moved on to the Colored Memorial School in Brunswick, which eventually had its name changed to Risley High School (see part IV). It is said that you can find an indentation in the ground about eighty feet away from the school building where one of the outhouse bathrooms once stood.[197] Some of the teachers of record were Mrs. Daisy (Mitchell) Waye, Arlie Baldwin and Mamie Hightower.[198]

In recent history, the school was converted into a home in the 1950s and is still used as such by family members,[199] but there have been considerations for converting the building back into a schoolhouse as a historic restoration project. On the Gilliard Farms property is a historical marker for the school that reads:

Gilliard Farms—Union School. *Matthew Raiford.*

This one room school house provided elementary education, grades kindergarten through eighth, to the Brookman Community from the year 1907 to 1955. This structure is an example of early African-American vernacular. In the early years of the school, one of the students, Mrs. Ophelia Johnson Killens, attended kindergarten through the fourth grade. Mrs. Killens has been the sole caretaker of the school since 1955. Some of the past teachers, according to the time frame were: Allie Baldwin, Gwendolyn Hankin, Ethel Chambers, Mamie Hightower, Elizabeth Roundtree, Donnie Mitchell, Mrs. Golsby and Daisy Waye. This historic marker has been donated by Mrs. Ofelia Johnson Killens and was dedicated in the year of our Lord, 2009.

PART VI

Concluding Thoughts, Heritage and the Future

In this final concluding chapter, we will discuss Gullah Geechee culture, heritage and history with a focus on how there can be a continuing inheritance in the Golden Isles. We address how these might be preserved for the future and why it is vitally important. And then we will also include some final thoughts.

Gullah Geechee culture is in serious danger of being lost from a variety of threats, including development, increasing property values and related swelling property taxes.[200] But the Gullah Geechee people are not going without a fight and are banding together to protect what is left of their beloved heritage.[201] Coastal development, growing property taxes, tourism, second homes and resort development are all eroding traditional Gullah Geechee culture and practices of farming, fishing and hunting at an extraordinary pace.[202] In some areas, a person's property taxes grew 1000 percent in just one year due to development.[203]

Displacement is a long and terrible process that is continuing to push the Gullah Geechee off their lands. Compounding this is something known as "heirs property," which stems from generations upon generations passing land down without clear deeds or other paperwork. Another issue is when a landowner dies and does not have a will to specify who would inherit the land.[204] Historically, there has been a deep distrust of government to obtain legal documents, or in some cases, none ever existed. Following seven, eight or nine generations of land passing down along a family line, a tract of land could have as many as one hundred people who claim right to it, which is known as fractional ownership.

Without proper documentation, landownership is tenuously held on to, and those who occupy the land have a number of legal issues and are often easily manipulated in situations where land is sold, they are evicted or land is taken with little recourse of action. At one time, following the Civil War, African Americans owned nearly twenty million acres of land, and today, many African Americans in rural areas still own large pieces of land.[205] Today, however, many of these people are unable to (or will not) use legal assistance because of income, distribution or distrust of the legal system.[206] Another consequence of fractional ownership is that a land developer might be able to purchase even one fraction of the land from an heir, which may then force a sale of the land or the land will be seized because of tax default.[207] A legal action known as partition means may be brought by a co-tenant, and as a result, a judge may sometimes order that the land be sold and the sale proceeds be divided among all those with a land interest.[208]

This means that those who lived and worked on the land for eight generations can be easily pushed off their land by anyone who can get even a tiny fraction of the land. This is a massive problem for the Gullah Geechee culture, as this type of predatory tactic is being used over and over by unscrupulous developers. There is work by the Gullah Geechee Cultural Heritage Corridor Commission, the St. Simons African American Heritage Coalition and the Sapelo Island Cultural and Revitalization Society, among others, to battle this in the state of Georgia, but it is an extremely difficult fight.

Sadly, much of the plight of the Gullah Geechee community is due to greed. Land developers use unsavory tactics to obtain land for much less than it's worth. Coupled with this may be ignorance of the buyers. The question is whether the buyers know that they've purchased a new home on land that belonged to freed slaves and their descendants for two centuries. And then if they did know, would they refuse to buy?

Unfortunately, this rapid development and greed is also destroying graveyards, sacred places and baptismal sites. In the South End of St. Simons Island, for instance, the entire community of twenty-seven buildings and associated landmarks was once proposed as a historic district but was also thought to be in peril because of new development in the area.[209]

The entire Harrington community, also on St. Simons Island, was once described as appropriate for the National Register of Historic Places. It was noted as the most intact of the three African American neighborhoods on

St. Simons Island. The description said, "The distinctive H-shaped pattern of the community's main streets, the rural, peaceful, historic setting of its coastal location, together with a broad collection of vernacular dwellings make Harrington an unrivaled and irreplaceable resource."[210] The same report warned that development would disrupt the historic setting of the community.

The great Cornelia Bailey of Sapelo Island, matriarch, keeper of the culture, author, storyteller and leader,[211] once wrote, "Yes, over the years we have forgotten most of the African ways, but even if there is only a tiny bit left, we celebrate it!"[212]

In the Golden Isles of Georgia, the heritage assets and heritage preservation of the Gullah Geechee have been discussed deeply among community leaders.[213] There are strong goals to identify all local heritage tourism assets with specificity to the African American and Gullah Geechee experiences for Glynn County and Brunswick. The impetus for these types of discussions was the need to both identify heritage tourism assets and to consider the ways to develop them in a sustainable and attractive fashion. Indeed, people here involved with Gullah Geechee communities share anecdotal evidence that strongly suggests that tourists to the area are interested in African American and Gullah Geechee heritage and culture in the region.

The state of Georgia tourism revenue generation has grown to nearly $60 billion.[214] Tourism in Glynn County and Brunswick has grown to receive 2.6 million visitors in 2016.[215] Tourism spending in Glynn County and Brunswick has grown to over $1 billion.[216] Heritage tourism is estimated to account for 40 percent of total international tourism, according to the World Tourism Organization, and could grow to a $90 billion opportunity by 2030.[217] Dr. J. Herman Blake, former executive director of the Gullah Geechee Cultural Heritage Corridor, says, "One of our general concerns beyond heritage tourism is the 'interpretation' of the cultures the tourists visit. The issues related to 'interpretation' require a multi-dimensional approach that gives serious consideration to those who reside in the communities where others visit. This subject is very complex and requires the visitor be aware of their cultural assumptions in viewing others."

A viable local heritage tourism product will not be possible without a complete assessment of the knowledge, skills, abilities and resources available. This will include identifying all relevant stakeholders; invitations for participation; identifying any history of collaboration or conflict; understanding power relationships; knowing ownership issues; forging commitments; filling skill gaps among stakeholders; and knowing the amount of money available and needed, the possible sources and the desired use (e.g. maintenance, development). To a degree, success will hinge on the people involved and the financial and human resources available.

A need for partnerships among the entities and stakeholders is needed to develop funding initiatives. Partnerships, such as public-private partnerships, are common for improving strategic outcomes and sustainability. Partnerships generally improve information flow, align interests and lower cultural boundaries. Positive collaborations stimulate sound planning, development, management, marketing and fundraising. There must be a framework for understanding what is necessary to have a successful local heritage tourism product. There must be commercial objectives and specific goals, even if a particular asset in the asset spectrum does not generate revenue. Consideration must be given to the components of successful heritage tourism, i.e., the attraction must tell a story, make the asset come alive (creative, entertaining interpretation), make the experience participatory, focus on quality and make it relevant to the tourist.

The sustainable development of African American and Gullah Geechee heritage tourism offers another positive reason for companies to consider establishing themselves in this area. The successful development of local heritage tourism will therefore have the potential for job creation, increased tax revenue and a stronger local economy.

The places people like to visit are also the places people like to live and work. Successful planning for heritage tourism should consider all opportunities. Another vital piece is a connection to the Gullah Geechee Cultural Heritage Corridor, which extends from Wilmington, North Carolina, to Jacksonville, Florida. The corridor promotes education, economic development and preservation of the culture and traditions of its namesake. Currently, there are only three Gullah Geechee sites recognized in Georgia: Pinpoint, Geechee Kunda and Sapelo. Effort is underway to incorporate assets in Glynn County and Brunswick such as the Harrington School.

As a "product," tourism is the largest industry in Glynn County and Brunswick. Concerns have been raised about attracting visitors here on heritage tourism trips. It was indicated that since this area is on a common route with places like Charleston, Savannah and St. Augustine, there is a need for better sustainable heritage tourism development to attract and retain heritage tourists. Culture and its connection to tourism essentially focuses on the landscapes, arts, traditions, music, food and religions of a region. This form of tourism can include events, museum visits, places of historical significance and interaction with locals. A cultural asset is an uncommodified or raw asset with intrinsic value. The task to develop the local heritage tourism product is to transform these raw assets into products for tourism consumption. There may be some trade-offs in the process as either cultural values are compromised for tourism use or tourism values are compromised for heritage conservation.

A cultural interest and experience discussed in this book is the Gullah Geechee foodways and the agriculture and historic "taste" specific to this region. A foodway is the eating habits and culinary practices of a people, region or historical period. In Georgia, historical African American influences on European cooking techniques and both Native American and introduced ingredients are noted to represent some of the most iconic dishes of the coast. It should be noted that slavery changed the foodways of the United States. Slavery, while being true to the terrible nature of the practice and history, is an important part of the local heritage story. Music is another dimension to local and historical culture. Another historical consideration is that Brunswick was one of the nation's original port cities.

Not all heritage assets will become successful local heritage tourism products. Successful products must be culturally significant, be able to withstand visitation/increased visitation, be able to attract/retain tourists and provide a quality experience. This generally involves planning, situation analyses, mission and vision establishment, goal setting, action plans, marketing and evaluation. There are, however, many extremely important Gullah Geechee heritage areas throughout the Golden Isles. These have been discussed at length in this book. The sites include places like Ibo Landing, where in 1803, captive Ibo people committed mass suicide in order to not submit to slavery. Gilliard Farms and the Union School is another, where seven generations of African Americans have owned, planted, harvested and partaken of food on this site. This site has a direct connection to both heritage and culture. From 1907 to 1955, the Union School on the site was the only one in the region to serve the educational needs of African American children.

The Historic Harrington School on St. Simons Island was built in the 1920s to educate the children of three African American communities on St. Simons Island; it was the only such school in the area. There is a need for more preservation of Brunswick sites like the Risley School and Selden Normal and Industrial Institute. The institute pioneered intermediate education of African Americans in the coastal area; it opened in 1903 and closed in 1933. The area is now a thirty-five-acre county park. The headmaster's cottage on the site could be restored as a cultural and educational center. Risley was originally the Colored Memorial School, which became Risley High School and is in the National Register of Historic Places.

The preservation of Gullah Geechee heritage in the Golden Isles is enormously important. A sustainable local heritage tourism product could bolster economic benefits to all stakeholders in the community. With fairly distributed employment and income-earning opportunities, local heritage tourism contributes to poverty alleviation. Indeed, in Brunswick, 37 percent of the population is below the poverty line. Unfortunately, historic neighborhoods and other historical assets are underutilized in this area. Engaging young people through employment as tour guides could help energize Gullah Geechee preservation and catalyze heritage education for new generations. In turn, this is an encouragement of entrepreneurship in local heritage, and from an economic standpoint, this would create more jobs. Youth engagement in creating local heritage tourism assets has implications for the newest generation to become grounded in local heritage because of ownership in the product development. Further, popular culture as a tool for intergenerational engagement, such as Beyoncé's music video for "Love Drought" that used imagery connected to Ibo Landing, could act as a bridge to a whole new generation of black youth.

In order to sustainably develop, maintain and protect the local Gullah Geechee heritage of the Golden Isles, this community must give strong consideration to human and financial capital, attraction of new businesses and tourists, authentic culture, historic interpretation, site development and cultural preservation, economic development issues and intergenerational engagement. We want to put an emphasis on education about local history, training for new tour guides, connections to agritourism and foodways, creating vibrancy and experiential opportunities, contributions to poverty alleviation, intergenerational engagement and the utilization of popular culture.

There are a multitude of ideas to help preserve local Gullah Geechee heritage, like designating historic neighborhoods, creating trolley tours with guides who are educated in Gullah Geechee heritage and engaging the knowledge of the local Gullah Geechee elders. Elders need to pass on the stories to the younger generations. There is a need to share oral histories and memories. There is a need to protect the properties that are threatened by loss. At some point, Gullah Geechee will be known as a cultural entity as opposed to just being a historical entity. Gullah Geechee people have something to express about themselves. It is not all doom and gloom; it is not about who Gullah Geechee were; it is not about the bad people who enslaved the West Africans—it is the hearts of who Gullah Geechee are as a community.

It will take both locals and visitors to come together to work to save this unique heritage. The West Africans who were enslaved and brought here against their will endured pain and suffering, as did their descendants. Humanity must stand together to recognize these sacrifices, protect an endangered culture and celebrate the heritage of the Gullah Geechee.

Amy Roberts's closing reflection:

> *The Gullah Geechee sites that are listed in this book are just the beginning. County-wide tours attempt to tell some of the history of the Golden Isles' Gullah Geechee heritage, yet few tours include stops at Gullah Geechee heritage sites. Yet very slowly, partnerships are beginning to grow. There is, for example, a partnership now between Fort Frederica National Monument and the Historic Harrington School. There is a celebration of the legacy of Robert Abbott and other entertainment at the fort and tours with heritage education and food at the Harrington School. In addition, at the Historic Harrington School there are monthly lectures open to the public that cover all sorts of areas of history, culture, heritage and the Gullah Geechee traditions of basket sewing, cooking and many others. This is a start. A start of opportunity for Gullah Geechee celebration and cultural continuation. A start in one place, on one island, in the midst of many more places that need similarly positive growth and outcomes built upon respect, community, goodwill, stewardship and love for one another. I do hope this book has given the reader a better understanding of the culture and heritage of the Gullah Geechee of the Golden Isles.*

NOTES

Part I

1. Vos, "Slave Trade from the Windward Coast," 29–51.
2. "Gold Coast," Encyclopedia Britannica.
3. "Gullah," Wikipedia.
4. Duthiers and Kermeliotis, "Slave Trade Ghost Town."
5. "Welcome," Gullah Geechee Cultural Heritage Corridor.
6. "Gullah/Geechee," National Park Service.
7. Morgan, *African American Life.*
8. "Resources," Gullah Geechee Cultural Heritage Corridor.
9. Feeser, *Red, White, and Black Make Blue.*
10. Crook, "Gullah-Geechee Archaeology," 1.
11. Ellis et al., "Qualitative Exploration of Fishing," 1161–70.
12. Hunt, *"My" Official Georgia Gullah Geechee Cookbook.*
13. "What Is a Basket? Fanner Baskets," National Museum of African Art.
14. "Gullah Geechee Food Traditions," Nourish.
15. "Basil Hall," Revolvy.
16. "Jollof Rice," Wikipedia.
17. "Sengalese Fish and Rice (Thieboudienne)," *Saveur.*
18. "Singing by Negroes in Unique Contest," *Brunswick News.*
19. "Call and Response," African Interactive.
20. Pollitzer, *Gullah People and Their African Heritage.*
21. Eligon, "About that Song You've Heard, Kumbaya."

22. "Recognizing the Song 'Kumbaya,'" Congressional Record.

23. "Ring Shout," Encyclopdedia.com.

24. Floyd, "Ring Shout!," 265–87.

25. Washington, "'Shabach Hallelujah!'"

26. Rosenbaum, *Shout Because You're Free.*

27. "Praise House," Gullah Community.

28. Simpson, "Shout and Shouting in Slave Religion," 34.

29. "Griot," Wikipedia.

30. National Park Service, "Low Country Gullah Culture Special Resource Study."

31. Bledsoe, "Marronage as a Past and Present Geography," 30–50.

32. Porter, *Black Seminoles.*

33. "Maroons," South Carolina Encyclopedia.

34. Opala, "Gullah: Rice, Slavery, and the Sierra Leone–American Connection."

35. Clark, *Hidden History of Florida.*

36. Opala, "Gullah: Rice, Slavery, and the Sierra Leone–American Connection."

37. Ibid.

38. Ibid.

39. "Public Law 109-338," United States Congress.

40. "Resources," Gullah Geechee Cultural Heritage Corridor.

41. "Order by the Commander of the Military Division of the Mississippi," Freedmen & Southern Society Project.

42. Marovich, "Can These Descendants of Enslaved Africans Save Their Unique Culture?"

43. National Park Service, "Low Country Gullah Culture Special Resource Study."

44. Faulkenberry, et al., "Culture of Servitude," 86–95.

45. Jarrett, "Connecting with the Soul of a Community."

46. Tate, "Georgia Sea Island Festival."

47. Rosenbaum and Downes, *Slave Songs of the Georgia Sea Islands.*

48. "Bessie Jones," National Endowment for the Arts.

49. "Alan Lomax Biography," American Folklife Center.

50. "Jim Brown," Wikipedia.

51. Schwartz, "Brown Was Hard to Bring Down."

52. Rushin, *Caddie Was a Reindeer.*

53. "Jim Brown," Wikipedia.

54. Hall, "Football Legend Still Calls St. Simons Island Home."

Part II

55. "Brunswick: Historical Overview," Institute of Southern Jewish Life.
56. Hobbs, "Prominent Black Newspaper Publisher's Roots on St. Simons."
57. "Charles Stevens," Oatland Plantation.
58. Zabar, "Chicago Defender's Silent Partner."
59. "Great Migration," *Fresh Air*.
60. "Lionel Hampton Biography," Biography.
61. "Glynn County Historic Resources Survey," Glynn County.
62. Asante and Mazama, *Encyclopedia of African Religion*.
63. "Chukwu," Wikipedia.
64. "Factual Basis of the Ebo Landing Legend," Biafra Nation.
65. S. Jones, this depiction of Neptune Small's story is found in the 1988 edition of the St. Simons Island Georgia Sea Island Heritage Festival program.
66. Cate, *Early Days of Coastal Georgia*.
67. Ibid.
68. "History," Epworth by the Sea.
69. Ibid.
70. "Tabby," New Georgia Encyclopedia.
71. Cate, *Early Days of Coastal Georgia*.
72. Ibid.
73. "Gould," Coastal Georgia Genealogy and History.
74. "Our History," First African Baptist Church.
75. "History," Christ Church Frederica.
76. Cate, *Early Days of Coastal Georgia*.
77. "Cannon's Point Preserve," St. Simons Land Trust.
78. Ibid.
79. Ibid.
80. "History," Christ Church Frederica.
81. Segedy, "Coastal Georgia Woman Becomes Episcopal Saint."
82. "Deaconess Alexander," Good Shepherd Episcopal Church.
83. Segedy, "Coastal Georgia Woman Becomes Episcopal Saint."
84. This history was found in a church publication in the records of the St. Simons African American Coalition.
85. Ibid.
86. "Liberty Ships," Golden Isles.
87. Hobbs, "Hazel's Café a Throwback."

Part III

88. "Sir Joseph Jekyll," Jekyll Island History.
89. "Dubignon Family," New Georgia Encyclopedia.
90. "Jekyll Island Authority," Jekyll Island.
91. "Wanderer Memory Trail Opening," Jekyll Island.
92. "The Slave Ship Wanderer," Jekyll Island Family Adventures.
93. "Memory Trail," Jekyll Island.
94. "Wanderer," New Georgia Encyclopedia.
95. Ibid.
96. "USS Wanderer," Wikipedia.
97. "MOSAIC Project Will Be Great Addition on Jekyll," *Brunswick News*.
98. Jones, "On Jekyll Island, Black History."
99. Bagwell, *Jekyll Island Club*.
100. Bagwell, "Jekyll Island Club," Jekyll Island History
101. Brock, "Lost Jekyll."
102. Bagwell, *Jekyll Island Club*.
103. Brock, "Lost Jekyll."
104. Chapman, "Chapel Visitors Fee."
105. Brown, "Origin (and Hot Stank) of the Chitlin Circuit."
106. Bagwell, "Triumphs and Challenges."
107. Ibid.
108. Bayliss, "Jekyll 4-H Center Transformed."
109. "Wilkes' Rites to Be Held on Monday." Glynn County, Georgia Archives.
110. Bagwell, "Triumphs and Challenges."
111. Ibid.
112. Glass-Hill, "Jim Bacote Dies."
113. Hobbs, "Memory Keepers."
114. "About Us," Geechee Kunda.
115. Glass-Hill, "Wa Jine We: Jim Bacote."
116. Demas, *Game of Privilege*.
117. Bagwell, "Triumphs and Challenges."
118. Allen, *Glynn County*.
119. "South End Community," Glynn County.
120. Wiggins and Swanson, *Separate Games*.
121. Bagwell, "Triumphs and Challenges."
122. Ibid.
123. Demas, *Game of Privilege*.
124. Ibid.

125. Bagwell, "Triumphs and Challenges."

126. Ibid.

127. Ibid.

Part IV

128. "Brunswick: Historical Overview," Institute of Southern Jewish Life.

129. Bagwell, "Opera House and Silent Movie Days of Brunswick."

130. Smith, *African American Theater Buildings*.

131. "Glynn County Tourism Product Development Report," Georgia Department of Economic Development.

132. Bagwell, "Opera House and Silent Movie Days of Brunswick."

133. Ibid.

134. "Roxy Theater," Cinema Treasures.

135. Starr, "Taking the Word to the Streets."

136. Bagwell, "Opera House and Silent Movie Days of Brunswick."

137. Barefoot, *Brunswick*.

138. "History of Selden Normal and Industrial Institute," Coastal Georgia Genealogy and History.

139. Short story of the life and work of Miss Carrie E. Bemus is found in a pamphlet in the records of the St. Simons African American Heritage Coalition.

140. "Glynn County Tourism Product Development Report," Georgia Department of Economic Development.

141. Ibid.

142. Bayliss, "Dixville Added to the Georgia Register of Historic Places."

143. "Icehouse History," Ice House Rock.

144. "City Commission Meeting Minutes," City of Brunswick.

145. Bayliss, "Dixville Added to the Georgia Register of Historic Places."

146. Summary of Proposed National Register/Georgia Register Nomination, Georgia Department of Natural Resources.

147. "Brookman Community," Coastal Georgia Genealogy and History.

148. "Glynn County Historic Resources Survey," Glynn County.

149. "Glynn County Tourism Product Development Report," Georgia Department of Economic Development.

150. "Glynn County Historic Resources Survey," Glynn County.

151. "Glynn County Tourism Product Development Report," Georgia Department of Economic Development.

152. Ibid.
153. "Greenwood," Coastal Georgia Genealogy and History.
154. "Oak Grove Cemetery," Discover Brunswick.

Part V

155. "Plantation & Slave History," Golden Isles.
156. Keeler, "Raised on Rice: Hofwyl-Broadfield Plantation."
157. Ibid.
158. "Hofwyl-Broadfield Plantation History," Lower Altamaha Historical Society.
159. Ibid.
160. "Hofwyl-Broadfield Plantation," Wikipedia.
161. Stewart, "Perseverance of a Plantation."
162. "Hofwyl-Broadfield Plantation," New Georgia Encyclopedia.
163. Ibid.
164. "Hofwyl-Broadfield Plantation," Slave Dwelling Project.
165. Ibid.
166. "Petersville/Broadfield Cemetery," Coastal Georgia Genealogy and History.
167. "Freedman's Rest," Coastal Georgia Genealogy and History.
168. Ibid.
169. "Petersville/Broadfield Cemetery," Coastal Georgia Genealogy and History.
170. "Needwood Baptist Church and School," Wikipedia.
171. Historic Rural Churches of Georgia.
172. Ibid.
173. Cate, *Early Days of Coastal Georgia*.
174. Ibid.
175. Hobbs, "Family Tree Grew Strong within Needwood Community."
176. Ibid.
177. "Episode 4—Slaves on the Coast," Saving Grace.
178. Hobbs, "Needwood Provides a Look Back."
179. Ibid.
180. Hobbs, "Family Tree Grew Strong within Needwood Community."
181. "Georgia Trust for Historic Preservation Announces Its 2019 List of State's 10 'Places in Peril,'" Georgia Trust for Historic Preservation.

182. "National Register of Historic Places Registration Form," National Park Service.
183. Chavis, "The Farmer & The Seeker."
184. Cyriaque, "Growing Food from Reconstruction to Organics."
185. Adkinson, "Brunswick Chef in Line for Major Award."
186. Cyriaque, "Growing Food from Reconstruction to Organics."
187. "We Farm Georgia," Georgia Organics.
188. Sessoms, "40 Acres & a Future."
189. Rhone, "Black Farmers in Georgia."
190. "Althea Raiford. Gilliard Farms, GA," Farmers Veteran Coalition.
191. Saulsbery, "Meet the Modern Farmer."
192. "Althea. Gilliard Farms," Kiva.
193. Twitty, *Cooking Gene*.
194. Roseboro, "Matthew Raiford."
195. Willis, *Secrets of the Southern Table*.
196. "Glynn County Historic Resources Survey," Glynn County.
197. "Union School," Coastal Georgia Genealogy and History.
198. Ibid.
199. Ibid.

Part VI

200. Suhay, "Real-Life 'Gullah Gullah Island' in Danger."
201. Jonsson, "Fight to Keep an Island's Black Heritage."
202. "Last of Its Kind," Grounds for Democracy.
203. Ibid.
204. "Unlocking Heir Property Ownership," Georgia Appleseed.
205. "What Is Heirs Property?" Heirs Property Retention Coalition.
206. Ibid.
207. Ibid.
208. "Unlocking Heir Property Ownership," Georgia Appleseed.
209. "Glynn County Historic Resources Survey," Glynn County.
210. Ibid.
211. Genzlinger, "Cornelia Bailey Dies."
212. Cornelia Bailey, "My Reflections," is found in the 1988 Georgia Sea Island Heritage Festival program, p. 12.
213. This is found in a report titled "Heritage Tourism Roundtable for Glynn County and Brunswick, GA."

214. "Tourism Industry Research," Georgia Department of Economic Development.
215. "Brunswick/Golden Isles," Georgia Trend.
216. Ibid.
217. "Valuing the SDG Prize," Business and Sustainable Development Commission.

Bibliography

Adkinson, Lyndsey. "Brunswick Chef in Line for Major Award." *Brunswick News*, February 21, 2018. thebrunswicknews.com/life/brunswick-chef-in-line-for-major-award/article_1de85f07-5c2b-5be8-9e47-3e56d6224a62.html.

African Interactive. "Call and Response." africaninteractive.org/projects/call-and-response.

Allen, Benjamin. *Glynn County, Georgia.* Charleston, SC: Arcadia Publishing, 2003.

The American Folklife Center. "Alan Lomax Biography." www.loc.gov/folklife/lomax/alanlomaxbio.html.

Asante, M., and A. Mazama. *Encyclopedia of African Religion.* Vol. 1. Thousand Oaks, CA: Sage, 2009.

Bagwell, Tyler E. *The Jekyll Island Club.* Charleston, SC: Arcadia Publishing, 1998.

———. "The Jekyll Island Club." Jekyll Island History. 2008. www.jekyllislandhistory.com/jckyllclub.shtml.

———. "The Opera House and Silent Movie Days of Brunswick." Jekyll Island History. www.jekyllislandhistory.com/theatres.shtml.

———. "Sir Joseph Jekyll: Master of the Rolls." Jekyll Island History. 2008. www.jekyllislandhistory.com/sirjosephjekyll.shtml.

———. "Triumphs and Challenges: The Segregation Years of Jekyll Island." Jekyll Island History. www.jekyllislandhistory.com/segregation.shtml.

Barefoot, P. *Brunswick: The City by the Sea*. Charleston, SC: Arcadia Publishing, 2000.

Bayliss, Deborah. "Dixville Added to the Georgia Register of Historic Places." *Brunswick News*, September 22, 2017. thebrunswicknews.com/news/local_news/dixville-added-to-georgia-register-of-historic-places/article_5db60f83-db6c-5d12-9aa3-678be3c16dbf.html.

———. "Jekyll 4-H Center Transformed into Camp Jekyll." *Brunswick News*, 2016. thebrunswicknews.com/news/local_news/jekyll--h-center-transformed-into-camp-jekyll/article_e5391e54-f438-554a-9a0a-322c951b70ea.html.

Biafra Nation. "The Factual Basis of the Ebo Landing Legend." www.biafraland.com/Igbo%20Landing,%20factual%20Basis.htm.

Biography. "Lionel Hampton Biography." www.biography.com/people/lionel-hampton-9327170.

Bledsoe, Adam. "Marronage as a Past and Present Geography in the Americas." *southeastern geographer* 57, no. 1 (2017): 30–50.

Brock, Wendell. "Lost Jekyll." trendmag2.trendoffset.com/publication/?i=497875&article_id=3091143&view=articleBrowser&ver=html5#{%22issue_id%22:497875,%22view%22:%22articleBrowser%22,%22article_id%22:%223091143%22}.

Brown, Tanya Ballard. "The Origin (and Hot Stank) of the Chitlin Circuit." 2014. www.npr.org/sections/codeswitch/2014/02/16/275313723/the-origin-and-hot-stank-of-the-chitlin-circuit.

Brunswick News. "MOSAIC Project Will Be Great Addition on Jekyll." thebrunswicknews.com/opinion/daily_editorial/mosaic-project-will-be-great-addition-on-jekyll/article_20b18786-7b7a-5f5a-87b9-b0fab01baa74.html.

———. "Singing by Negroes in Unique Contest." 1935.

Business and Sustainable Development Commission. "Valuing the SDG Prize: Unlocking Business Opportunities to Accelerate Sustainable and Inclusive Growth." 2017. s3.amazonaws.com/aws-bsdc/Valuing-the-SDG-Prize.pdf.

Cate, Margaret Davis. *Early Days of Coastal Georgia*. N.p.: Fort Frederica Association, 1955.

Chapman, Dan. "Chapel Visitors Fee Makes Waves at Jekyll Island." *Atlantic Journal Constitution*, January 15, 2016. www.ajc.com/news/state--regional-govt--politics/chapel-visitors-fee-makes-waves-jekyll-island/mqJ6ap5i3uhZPulua4ecuN.

Chavis, Shaun. "The Farmer & The Seeker." *Peach Dish*, August 8, 2017. www.peachdish.com/blog/WYoQLyYAAN-kd58l/the-farmer--the-seeker.

Christ Church Frederica. "History." 2018. ccfssi.org/about-us/21-about-us/about/74-history.html.

Cicuivich, R. "Glynn County Historic Resources Survey Report." 2009. www.glynncounty.org/DocumentCenter/View/9254/2009_Glynn_Co-_HRS_Report2?bidId=.

Cinema Treasures. "Roxy Theater." cinematreasures.org/theaters/16502.

City of Brunswick. "City Commission Meeting Minutes." July 7, 2004. www.brunswickga.org/2004/07-07-2004.PDF.

Clark, James C. *Hidden History of Florida*. Charleston, SC: The History Press, 2015.

Cleveland, Jean. "Hofwyl-Broadfield Plantation." New Georgia Encyclopedia. September 15, 2014. www.georgiaencyclopedia.org/articles/history-archaeology/hofwyl-broadfield-plantation.

Coastal Georgia Genealogy and History. "Brookman Community." 2018. www.glynngen.com/history/brookman.htm.

———. "Freedman's Rest." www.glynngen.com/cemetery/glynn/freedmans.

———. "Gould." www.glynngen.com/cemetery/glynn/gould.

———. "Greenwood." 2017. www.glynngen.com/cemetery/glynn/greenwood.

———. "History of Selden Normal and Industrial Institute." www.glynncounty.com/oaktree.pl?id=00013035.

———. "Petersville/Broadfield Cemetery." 2018. www.glynngen.com/cemetery/glynn/petersville.

———. "Union School." www.glynngen.com/schools/glynn/union.

Congressional Record. "Recognizing the Song 'Kumbaya.'" 2017. www.congress.gov/congressional-record/2017/12/07/house-section/article/H9714-1.

Crook, Ray. "Gullah-Geechee Archaeology: The Living Space of Enslaved Geechee on Sapelo Island." *African Diaspora Archaeology Newsletter* 11, no. 1 (2008): 1.

Cyriaque, Jeanne. "Growing Food from Reconstruction to Organics: Gilliard Farms, an African American Centennial Farm." *Reflections*, December 2012. georgiashpo.org/sites/default/files/hpd/pdf/AfricanAmericanHistoricPlaces/December%202012.pdf.

de los Santos, Penny. "Sengalese Fish and Rice (Thieboudienne)." *Saveur*, 2002. www.saveur.com/article/Recipes/Senegal-Fish-Rice.

Demas, Lane. *Game of Privilege: An African American History of Golf*. Chapel Hill: University of North Carolina Press, 2017.

Discover Brunswick. "Oak Grove Cemetery." 2015. discoverbrunswick.com/images/Oak-Grove-Brochure.pdf.

Duthiers, Vladmir, and Teo Kermeliotis. "Slave Trade Ghost Town: The Dark History of Bunce Island." CNN, May 16, 2013. www.cnn.com/2013/05/16/world/africa/bunce-island-slavery-west-africa/index.html.

Eligon, J. "About that Song You've Heard, Kumbaya." *New York Times*, February 9, 2018. www.nytimes.com/2018/02/09/us/kumbaya-gullah-geechee.html.

Ellis, J.H., D.B. Friedman, R. Puett, G.I. Scott and D.E. Porter. "A Qualitative Exploration of Fishing and Fish Consumption in the Gullah/Geechee Culture." *Journal of Community Health* 39, no. 6 (2014): 1161–70.

Encyclopedia Britannica. "Gold Coast, Historical Region, Africa." 1998. www.britannica.com/place/Gold-Coast-historical-region-Africa.

Encyclopedia.com. "The Ring Shout." www.encyclopedia.com/humanities/applied-and-social-sciences-magazines/ring-shout.

Epworth by the Sea. "History." epworthbythesea.org/history.

Farmers Veteran Coalition. "Althea Raiford. Gilliard Farms, GA." www.farmvetco.org/stories/althea-raiford.

Faulkenberry, Lisa V., John M. Coggeshall, Kenneth Backman and Sheila Backman. "A Culture of Servitude: The Impact of Tourism and Development on South Carolina's Coast." *Human Organization* (2000): 86–95.

Feeser, Andrea. *Red, White, and Black Make Blue: Indigo in the Fabric of Colonial South Carolina Life.* Athens: University of Georgia Press, 2013.

First African Baptist Church. "Our History." www.fabsaintsimons.org/Our-History.

Fitzgerald, Catherine. "Maroons." South Carolina Encyclopedia. 2016. www.scencyclopedia.org/sce/entries/maroons.

Floyd, Samuel A. "Ring Shout! Literary Studies, Historical Studies, and Black Music Inquiry." *Black Music Research Journal* (1991): 265–87.

Freedmen & Southern Society Project. "Order by the Commander of the Military Division of the Mississippi." 2017. www.freedmen.umd.edu/sfo15.htm.

Fresh Air. "Great Migration: The African American Exodus North." 2010. www.npr.org/templates/story/story.php?storyId=129827444.

Geechee Kunda. "About Us." www.geecheekunda.com/about.htm.

Genzlinger, Neil. "Cornelia Bailey, Champion of African-Rooted Culture in Coastal Georgia, Dies at 72." *New York Times*, October 18, 2017. www.nytimes.com/2017/10/18/obituaries/cornelia-bailey-champion-of-african-rooted-culture-in-coastal-georgia-dies-at-72.html.

Georgia Appleseed. "Unlocking Heir Property Ownership: Assessing the Impact on Low and Mid-Income Georgians and Their Communities." 2013. gaappleseed.org/media/docs/unlocking-heir-property.pdf.

Georgia Department of Economic Development. "Glynn County Tourism Product Development Report." 2017. www.marketgeorgia.org/resource/glynn-county-tourism-product-development-report.

———. "Tourism Industry Research." 2017. www.georgia.org/industries/georgia-tourism/industry-research.

Georgia Department of Natural Resources. Summary of Proposed National Register/Georgia Register Nomination. 2017. gadnr.org/sites/default/files/hpd/pdf/Dixville%20Historic%20District_Summary.pdf.

Georgia Organics. "We Farm Georgia—Matthew Raiford, Gilliard Farm." 2016. vimeo.com/140433701.

Georgia Trend. "Brunswick/Golden Isles: Optimism Abounds." 2016. www.georgiatrend.com/June-2016/Brunswick-Golden-Isles-Optimism-Abounds.

The Georgia Trust for Historic Preservation. "Georgia Trust for Historic Preservation Announces Its 2019 List of State's 10 'Places in Peril.'" 2018. www.georgiatrust.org/press-releases/2019-places-in-peril.

Glass-Hill, H. "Jim Bacote, Engine Driving Gullah Geechee Center, Dies." Coastal Courier, May 11, 2018. coastalcourier.com/news/jim-bacote-engine-driving-gullah-geechee-center-dies.

———. "Wa Jine We: Jim Bacote (1948–2018)." Savannah Tribune, May 16, 2018. www.savannahtribune.com/articles/wa-jine-we-jim-bacote-1948-2018.

Glynn County. "South End Community." 2012. www.glynncounty.com/oaktree.pl?id=00012724.

Glynn County, Georgia. "Glynn County Historic Resources Survey." www.glynncounty.org/DocumentCenter/View/9254/2009_Glynn_Co-_HRS_Report2?bidId=.

———. "The History of Selden Normal and Industrial Institute." 2012. www.glynncounty.com/oaktree.pl?id=00013035.

Glynn County, Georgia Archives. "Wilkes Rites to Be Held on Monday." 2006. files.usgwarchives.net/ga/glynn/obits/w/wilkes3610gob.txt.

Golden Isles. "Liberty Ships." 2018. www.goldenisles.com/discover/golden-isles/history-and-heritage/liberty-ships.

Golden Isles Georgia. "Plantation & Slave History." 2019. www.goldenisles.com/discover/golden-isles/african-american-heritage/plantation-slavery-history.

Good Shepherd Episcopal Church. "Deaconess Alexander." 2011. goodshepherdbrunswick.georgiaepiscopal.org/?page_id=8.

Grounds for Democracy. "Last of Its Kind: The Vanishing Landscapes of the Gullah Geechee." 2018. tclf.org/sites/default/files/microsites/landslide2018/hog-hammock.html.

Gullah Community. "Praise House." 2018. gullahcommunity.org/our-community/praise-house.

Gullah Geechee Cultural Heritage Corridor. "Welcome." 2018. www.gullahgeecheecorridor.org.

Gullah Geechee Cultural Heritage Corridor Commission. Gullah Geechee Cultural Heritage Corridor Management Plan. Prepared and published by the National Park Service, Denver Service Center, 2012.

Hall, Michael. "Football Legend Still Calls St. Simons Island Home." 2014. thebrunswicknews.com/news/local_news/football-legend-still-calls-st-simons-island-home/article_02262f1e-a83e-5b03-b7dc-7a22da2716b2.html.

Heirs Property Retention Coalition. "What Is Heirs Property?" southerncoalition.org/hprc/?q=node/5.

Historic Rural Churches of Georgia. 2019. www.hrcga.org/county/glynn.

Hobbs, Larry. "Family Tree Grew Strong within Needwood Community." Brunswick News, May 5, 2018. thebrunswicknews.com/news/local_news/family-tree-grew-strong-within-needwood-community/article_e7cc3ce1-351a-58fc-96fb-21b123ccf8d2.html.

———. "Hazel's Café a Throwback to the Island's Past." Brunswick News, September 28, 2018. thebrunswicknews.com/news/local_news/hazel-s-cafe-a-throwback-to-island-s-past/article_d0e6d160-2819-5936-beaf-2908f161af69.html.

———. "The Memory Keepers." Golden Isles, June 26, 2015. www.goldenislesmagazine.com/features/the-memory-keepers/article_8b16b164-1682-11e5-b366-d3d73ba0ff35.html.

———. "Needwood Provides a Look Back at Local Black History—For Now." Brunswick News, May 2, 2018. thebrunswicknews.com/news/local_news/needwood-provides-a-look-back-at-local-black-history-for/article_e4550f82-21bd-5924-b5a8-5b84854c8644.html.

———. "Prominent Black Newspaper Publisher's Roots on St. Simons." Brunswick News, February 17, 2018. thebrunswicknews.com/news/local_news/prominent-black-newspaper-publisher-s-roots-on-st-simons/article_cfa774b8-80e2-5da2-8b9b-485f7f20fc89.html.

Hunt, S.K. "My" Official Georgia Gullah Geechee Cookbook: Geechees, Low Country Cooking and History Facts. Bloomington, IN: Xlibris, 2015.

Ice House Rock. "Icehouse History." 2007. www.icehouserock.com/history.html.

Institute of Southern Jewish Life. "Brunswick: Historical Overview." 2017. www.isjl.org/georgia-brunswick-encyclopedia.html.

Jarrett, C. "Connecting with the Soul of a Community: An Interactive Study of Gullah Culture." *Black Praxis*, 2003.

Jekyll Island. "Jekyll Island Authority." 2018. www.jekyllisland.com/jekyll-island-authority.

———. "A Memory Trail—The Story of the Survivors of the Slave Ship Wanderer through a Family Learning Experience." 2018. www.jekyllisland.com/jekyllislandwp/wp-content/uploads/2016/01/Memory-Trail.pdf.

———. "The Wanderer Memory Trail Opening Ceremony." www.jekyllisland.com/event/the-wanderer-memory-trail-opening-ceremony

Jekyll Island Family Adventures. "The Slave Ship Wanderer—A Tale of Courage and Adversity." 2018. www.jekyll-island-family-adventures.com/slave-ship-wanderer.html.

Jones, Tyler H. "On Jekyll Island, Black History Remains Prominent." *Brunswick News*, February 3, 2017. thebrunswicknews.com/life/on-jekyll-island-black-history-remains-prominent/article_3272b285-ee8e-5f5a-a7c7-a0683a9bbb6f.html.

Jonsson, Patrik. "A Fight to Keep an Island's Black Heritage." *Christian Science Monitor*, January 29, 2002. www.csmonitor.com/2002/0129/p03s01-ussc.html.

Keber, Martha L. "Dubignon Family." 2003. www.georgiaencyclopedia.org/articles/history-archaeology/Dubignon-family.

Keeler, Jane. "Raised on Rice: The Hofwyl-Broadfield Plantation." Porter Briggs: The Voice of the South. porterbriggs.com/raised-on-rice-the-hofwyl-broadfield-plantation.

Kiva. "Althea. Gilliard Farms." 2016. www.kiva.org/lend/1090563.

Lower Altamaha Historical Society. "Hofwyl-Broadfield Plantation History." www.loweraltamahahistoricalsociety.org/community/Hofwyl_Broadfield_History.htm.

Marovich, Pete. "Can These Descendants of Enslaved Africans Save Their Unique Culture?" *Washington Post*, 2018. www.washingtonpost.com/graphics/2018/lifestyle/magazine/amp-stories/gullah-geechee-culture-south-carolina.

McGill, Joseph. "Hofwyl-Broadfield Plantation." The Slave Dwelling Project, June 5, 2015. slavedwellingproject.org/hofwyl-broadfield-plantation.

Morgan, Philip, ed. *African American Life in the Georgia Lowcountry: The Atlantic World and the Gullah Geechee.* Athens: University of Georgia Press, 2011.

National Endowment for the Arts. "Bessie Jones." www.arts.gov/honors/heritage/fellows/bessie-jones.

National Museum of African Art. "What Is a Basket? Fanner Baskets."
africa.si.edu/exhibits/grassroots/fanner.html.

National Park Service. "Gullah/Geechee." www.nps.gov/guge/learn/
historyculture/people.htm.

———. "Low Country Gullah Culture Special Resource Study and
Final Environmental Impact Statement." Atlanta, GA: NPS Southeast
Regional Office, 2005.

———. "National Register of Historic Places Registration Form." 1998.
https://npgallery.nps.gov/GetAsset/4cde88a7-0984-4c6f-870d-
90e1cf65ec64.

New Georgia Encyclopedia. "Dubignon Family." www.
georgiaencyclopedia.org/articles/history-archaeology/Dubignon-family.

———. "Hofwyl-Broadfield Plantation." www.georgiaencyclopedia.org/
articles/history-archaeology/hofwyl-broadfield-plantation.

———. "Tabby." www.georgiaencyclopedia.org/articles/history-
archaeology/tabby.

———. "Wanderer." www.georgiaencyclopedia.org/articles/history-
archaeology/wanderer.

Nourish. "Gullah Geechee Food Traditions." YouTube. www.youtube.
com/watch?v=bvUUgNFYVNk.

Oatland Plantation. "Charles Stevens." www.oatland.org/Photo_Gallery/
Charles_Stevens.htm.

Opala, Joseph. "The Gullah: Rice, Slavery, and the Sierra Leone–
American Connection. Freetown." Sierra Leone, United States
Information Service (1987).

Pollitzer, William S. *The Gullah People and Their African Heritage.* Athens:
University of Georgia Press, 2005.

Porter, Kenneth Wiggins. *The Black Seminoles: History of a Freedom-Seeking
People.* Gainesville: University Press of Florida, 1996.

Revolvy. "Basil Hall." www.revolvy.com/page/Basil-Hall.

Rhone, Nedra. "Black Farmers in Georgia Reclaiming Agricultural
Roots." *Atlanta Journal-Constitution*, August 29, 2018. www.ajc.com/
blog/talk-town/black-farmers-georgia-reclaiming-agricultural-roots/
WM20O5kYme6c7MtsCjgSnL.

Rohrer, K.E. "Wanderer." Georgia Encyclopedia, 2010. www.
georgiaencyclopedia.org/articles/history-archaeology/wanderer.

Roseboro, Ken. "Matthew Raiford: Sixth Generation Georgia Farmer,
Award Winning Chef." *The Organic and Non-GMO Report*, April 3, 2018.
non-gmoreport.com/articles/matthew-raiford-sixth-generation-georgia-
farmer.

Rosenbaum, Art. *Shout Because You're Free: The African American Ring Shout Tradition in Coastal Georgia.* Athens: University of Georgia Press, 2012.

Rosenbaum, Art, and Olin Downes. *Slave Songs of the Georgia Sea Islands.* Athens: University of Georgia Press, 1992.

Rushin, Steve. *The Caddie Was a Reindeer: And Other Tales of Extreme Recreation.* New York: Grove Press, 2004.

Saulsbery, Gabrielle. "Meet the Modern Farmer: Military Veteran Edition." *Modern Farmer,* May 25, 2015. modernfarmer.com/2015/05/meet-the-modern-farmer-military-veteran-edition.

Saving Grace. "Episode 4—Slaves on the Coast, Evolution on Trial & Catholics in GA." 2018. www.gpb.org/television/shows/saving-grace/episode/aed2bf6b-3d8e-4e51-a0df-0f987b772a30.

Schwartz, Larry. "Brown Was Hard to Bring Down." ESPN. www.espn.com/sportscentury/features/00014125.html.

Segedy, A. "Coastal Georgia Woman Becomes Episcopal Saint." Savannah Now, July 13, 2018. www.savannahnow.com/entertainmentlife/20180713/coastal-georgia-woman-becomes-episcopal-saint.

Sessoms, Eileen Mouyard. "40 Acres & a Future." *Savannah Magazine,* May 10, 2017. www.savannahmagazine.com/40-acres-future.

Simpson, Robert. "The Shout and Shouting in Slave Religion of the United States." *Southern Quarterly* 23, no. 3 (1985): 34.

Slave Dwelling Project. "Hofwyl-Broadfield Plantation." slavedwellingproject.org/hofwyl-broadfield-plantation.

Smith, Eric Ledell. *African American Theater Buildings: An Illustrated Historical Directory, 1900–1955.* New York: McFarland, 2015.

Starr, Mary. "Taking the Word to the Streets, and Bringing Unity to the Community." *Brunswick News,* July 15, 2017. thebrunswicknews.com/life/taking-the-word-to-the-streets-and-bringing-unity-to/article_e5330167-4486-5792-ad51-80cbdb1d4785.html.

Stewart, Mason. "Perseverance of a Plantation." *Elegant Island Living,* December 27, 2015. www.elegantislandliving.net/ssi-archives/perseverance-of-a-plantation.

St. Simons Land Trust. "Cannon's Point Preserve." www.sslt.org/index.php/cannon-s-point.

Suhay, Lisa. "Real-Life 'Gullah Gullah Island' in Danger." *Christian Science Monitor,* October 2, 2013. www.csmonitor.com/The-Culture/Family/Modern-Parenthood/2013/1002/Real-life-Gullah-Gullah-Island-in-danger.

Tate, Brittany. "Georgia Sea Island Festival." *Brunswick News,* June 3, 2016. thebrunswicknews.com/life/georgia-sea-island-festival/article_5c244464-14d3-5bbe-857d-f078c0d5df6c.html.

Twitty, Michael. *The Cooking Gene: A Journey Through African-American Culinary History in the Old South.* New York: Amistad, 2017.

United States Congress. (2006). Public Law 109-338. www.congress. gov/109/plaws/publ338/PLAW-109publ338.pdf.

Vos, Jelmer. "The Slave Trade from the Windward Coast: The Case of the Dutch, 1740–1805." *African Economic History* 38, no. 1 (2010): 29–51.

Washington, Erica Lanice. "'Shabach Hallelujah!': The Continuity of the Ring Shout Tradition as a Site of Music and Dance in Black American Worship." PhD diss., Bowling Green State University, 2005.

Wiggins, David K., and Ryan A. Swanson. *Separate Games: African American Sport behind the Walls of Segregation.* Fayetteville: University of Arkansas Press, 2016.

Wikipedia. "Chukwu." en.wikipedia.org/wiki/Chukwu.

———. "Gullah." en.wikipedia.org/wiki/Gullah#African_roots.

———. "Hofwyl-Broadfield Plantation." en.wikipedia.org/wiki/Hofwyl-Broadfield_Plantation.

———. "Jim Brown." en.wikipedia.org/wiki/Jim_Brown#Early_life.

———. "Jim Brown." en.wikipedia.org/wiki/Jim_Brown#Professional_football_career.

———. "Jollof Rice." en.wikipedia.org/wiki/Jollof_rice.

———. "Needwood Baptist Church and School." cn.wikipcdia.org/wiki/Needwood_Baptist_Church_and_School.

———. "USS Wanderer." en.wikipedia.org/wiki/USS_Wanderer_(1857).

Willis, Virginia. *Secrets of the Southern Table: A Food Lover's Tour of the Global South.* New York: Houghton Mifflin Harcourt, 2018.

Wolfe, W. "Wanderer Memory Trail Opens on Saturday." *Brunswick News*, November 16, 2018. thebrunswicknews.com/news/local_news/wanderer-memory-trail-opens-saturday/article_7f422c65-4213-5297-9ab1-9fb8fff331bb.html.

Zabar, Kai El. "The Chicago Defender's Silent Partner." 2014. chicagodefender.com/2016/05/11/the-chicago-defenders-silent-partner.

SUGGESTIONS FOR
ADDITIONAL READING

Allen, Benjamin. *Glynn County, Georgia*. Charleston, SC: Arcadia Publishing, 2003.

Austin, Allan D. *African Muslims in Antebellum America: Transatlantic Stories and Spiritual Struggles*. Abingdon, UK: Routledge, 2012.

Bagwell, Tyler E. *The Jekyll Island Club*. Charleston, SC: Arcadia Publishing, 1998.

Bailey, Cornelia Walker. *God, Dr. Buzzard, and the Bolito Man*. New York: Anchor Books, 2001.

Bell, Malcolm, Jr. *Major Butler's Legacy: Five Generations of a Slaveholding Family*. Athens: University of Georgia Press, 2004.

Brown, Alphonso. *A Gullah Guide to Charleston: Walking Through Black History*. Charleston, SC: The History Press, 2008.

Cross, Wilbur. *Gullah Culture in America*. Westport, CT: Greenwood Publishing Group, 2008.

Doster, Stephen. *Voices from St. Simons: Personal Narratives of an Island's Past*. New York: Blair, 2008.

Georgia Writers' Project. *Drums and Shadows: Survival Studies among the Georgia Coastal Negroes*. Athens: University of Georgia Press, 1940.

Hess, Karen, and Robert M. Weir. *The Carolina Rice Kitchen: The African Connection*. Columbia: University of South Carolina Press, 1992.

Jones, Bessie, and Bess Lomax Hawes. *Step It Down: Games, Plays, Songs, and Stories from the Afro-American Heritage*. Athens: University of Georgia Press, 1987.

King, Anna Matilda. *Anna: The Letters of a St. Simons Island Plantation Mistress, 1817–1859*. Athens: University of Georgia Press, 2010.

Morgan, Philip D., and Richard Newman, eds. *African American Life in the Georgia Lowcountry: The Atlantic World and the Gullah Geechee*. Athens: University of Georgia Press, 2010.

Turner, Lorenzo Dow, Michael Montgomery and Katherine Wyly Mille. *Africanisms in the Gullah Dialect*. Chicago: University of Chicago Press, 1949.

INDEX

About the Authors

Amy Roberts is the executive director of the St. Simons African American Heritage Coalition and has been an island tour guide for more than twenty years. Amy was born and raised on St. Simons Island and is a direct descendant of enslaved West Africans who were brought to the Golden Isles on the *Wanderer* slave ship. Amy is deeply involved with her community and is the recipient of a number of awards, including the Georgia Governor's Award for the Arts and Humanities, the NAACCP Image Award and the Golden Isles Hospitality Shared Vision Award.

Patrick Holladay is an academic, researcher and writer whose main research revolves around sustainability, resilience and community development. Patrick is highly involved with a number of professional and community groups and is the president of the Friends of the Harrington School, which is the support organization for the St. Simons African American Heritage Coalition.

Visit us at
www.historypress.com